William Damon, *Brown University*
EDITOR-IN-CHIEF

Cultural Practices as Contexts for Development

Jacqueline J. Goodnow
Macquarie University, Sydney

Peggy J. Miller
University of Illinois, Urbana–Champaign

Frank Kessel
Social Science Research Council

EDITORS

Number 67, Spring 1995

JOSSEY-BASS PUBLISHERS
San Francisco

CULTURAL PRACTICES AS CONTEXTS FOR DEVELOPMENT
Jacqueline J. Goodnow, Peggy J. Miller, Frank Kessel (eds.)
New Directions for Child Development, no. 67
William Damon, Editor-in-Chief

Microfilm copies of issues and articles are available in 16mm and 35mm, as well as microfiche in 105mm, through University Microfilms Inc., 300 North Zeeb Road, Ann Arbor, Michigan 48106-1346.

LC 85-644581   ISSN 0195-2269   ISBN 0-7879-9915-6

NEW DIRECTIONS FOR CHILD DEVELOPMENT is part of The Jossey-Bass Education Series and is published quarterly by Jossey-Bass Inc., Publishers, 350 Sansome Street, San Francisco, California 94104-1342 (publication number USPS 494-090). Second-class postage paid at San Francisco, California, and at additional mailing offices. POSTMASTER: Send address changes to Jossey-Bass Inc., Publishers, 350 Sansome Street, San Francisco, California 94104-1342.

EDITORIAL CORRESPONDENCE should be sent to the Editor-in-Chief, William Damon, Department of Education, Box 1938, Brown University, Providence, Rhode Island 02912.

Cover photograph by Wernher Krutein/PHOTOVAULT © 1990.

Manufactured in the United States of America. Nearly all Jossey-Bass books, jackets, and periodicals are printed on recycled paper that contains at least 50 percent recycled waste, including 10 percent postconsumer waste. Many of our materials are also printed with vegetable-based inks; during the printing process these inks emit fewer volatile organic compounds (VOCs) than petroleum-based inks. VOCs contribute to the formation of smog.

CONTENTS

EDITORS' NOTES

Although the terms *context* and *culture* are by no means newcomers to the discourse of developmental psychology, they have been moving, in recent years, from the margins toward the center of the discipline. In part, this reflects growing recognition of the enormous variation in the conditions under which "normal" development proceeds both within and across societies. It also reflects increasing awareness that for children everywhere—including those in our own backyards—development is an outgrowth of cultural life and thus is inextricably bound to particular contexts. This emerging sense of the inseparability of development and cultures is expressed in a variety of ways. More and more we hear that development is situated, that contexts are inherently dynamic, that children and cultures are co-constituted.

In this volume, we examine a promising approach to the study of development-in-context—one that is grounded in the notion of cultural practices. Cultural practices are meaningful actions that occur routinely in everyday life, are widely shared by members of the group, and carry with them normative expectations about how things should be done. In recent years, practice theories have had a major impact on thinking in sociology and anthropology. At the same time, developmentalists have turned to this idea because it offers a unified view of development and culture as intertwined processes as well as fresh insights into the problem of how development comes about. The question that arose for us is, How is the notion of cultural practices being translated into research?

This volume brings together several research initiatives undertaken from a practice perspective. Our aim is to illustrate the conceptual and methodological innovations prompted by this approach as they are instantiated in specific studies. The volume grew out of a symposium on Cultural Practices as Contexts for Development at the biennial meeting of the Society for Research in Child Development (SRCD) in March 1992 and a workshop on the same topic convened by the editors under the sponsorship of the Social Science Research Council's (SSRC) Committee on Culture, Health, and Human Development.

The workshop took place in New Orleans immediately after the SRCD meeting and was made possible by a much-appreciated Officer's Discretionary Grant from the William T. Grant Foundation. Via its explicitly exploratory agenda and the participation of members of the Committee of Culture, Health, and Human Development and other scholars (from the Committee's Program on Cultural Constructions of Human Development), the workshop exemplified the SSRC's commitment to the shaping and sharpening of interdisciplinary discussion. The participants were Margarita Azmitia, Michael Cole, Catherine Cooper, Jacqueline Goodnow, Sara Harkness, Giyoo Hatano, Kayoko Inagaki, Frank Kessel, Don Kulick, Barbara Miller, Peggy Miller, Terezinha Nunes,

Elinor Ochs, Barbara Rogoff, Bambi Schiefflin, Robert Serpell, Richard Shweder, and Carol Worthman. (For general background on the Committee's work, which is supported by the MacArthur Foundation, see Kessel, 1992).

The contributors to the volume are developmentalists (with disciplinary homes in psychology and anthropology) who have studied a variety of cultural practices. In their study of sleeping arrangements in American and Hindu families, Richard Shweder, Lene Arnett Jensen, and William Goldstein take up the question, How can the researcher identify the principles that may be unarticulated in a particular practice? Barbara Rogoff, Jacqueline Baker-Sennett, Pilar Lacasa, and Denise Goldsmith illustrate how a cultural practices approach transforms our understanding of the developmental process. The practice that they examine is Girl Scout cookie sales. Barbara Miller addresses the situation that arises when adolescents find themselves involved in conflicting practices—those of their Hindu immigrant parents and those of their American high school peer group. Terezinha Nunes starts from the question, How does the nature of the activity influence the nature of what is acquired? She grounds this question in research on the use of everyday arithmetic strategies. Michael Cole, whose groundbreaking work on sociohistorical theory presaged many of the issues addressed here, places the preceding chapters in their historical context. He discusses the variety of terms—*practice, activity, event, context*—commonly in use for specifying a unit of analysis that is larger than but inclusive of the individual.

The organization of the volume follows from our goal of clarifying, assessing, and enhancing the usefulness of a cultural practices approach. The opening chapter provides the substantive framework for the volume, delineating a set of propositions about the nature and developmental role of cultural practices. Each of the succeeding chapters takes up one or more of these propositions as illustrated in the authors' own research. Brief editorial commentary at the beginning of Chapters Two through Five links the study discussed in each to other research concerned with similar problems and underscores conceptual and methodological innovations. The volume concludes with Michael Cole's discussion and with a conclusion that identifies issues and directions for the future.

Jacqueline J. Goodnow
Peggy J. Miller
Frank Kessel
Editors

Reference

Kessel, F. "On Culture, Health, and Human Development: Emerging Perspectives." *Items,* 1992, *46*(4), 65–72.

JACQUELINE J. GOODNOW is *professorial research fellow, School of Behavioral Sciences, Macquarie University, Sydney.*

PEGGY J. MILLER is *associate professor, Department of Speech Communication and Department of Psychology, University of Illinois, Urbana–Champaign.*

FRANK KESSEL is *program director, Social Science Research Council, with major responsibility for the Committee on Culture, Health, and Human Development.*

This chapter explains why the notion of cultural practices has been appealing to developmental researchers and introduces the conceptual framework for the volume.

Cultural Practices: Toward an Integration of Culture and Development

Peggy J. Miller, Jacqueline J. Goodnow

Cultural practices are currently a prominent topic in many fields: anthropology, sociology, feminist studies, linguistic studies. Our focus in this volume will be upon implications for analyses of development, with a particular emphasis upon the question, How are ideas about practices being translated into developmental research?

Each of the interior chapters has its own preface, geared to the specific issues that the chapter addresses. The general introduction provided in this chapter is relevant to all of the chapters. It asks why developmentalists have come to be interested in the concept of practices, provides a minimal background, raises questions of definition, outlines the propositions that the chapters explore, and anchors these within a single content area. The later chapters draw upon a variety of content areas. In this introductory chapter, however, we restrict ourselves to studies of language, both for coherence and in recognition of the way this content area has contributed both concepts and methods to the study of practices. We draw especially from studies of language socialization—a tradition that rests on the assumption that language, conceived as discursive practices, is the primary tool by which children are socialized into valued ways of acting, thinking, and feeling.

Definition of the Term *Cultural Practices*

What does the term *cultural practices* refer to, and what precisely does it offer? From the start, we need to say that there is no single definition—a lack of uniformity that is not surprising when we consider Ortner's statement that practice is the "new key symbol" around which theoretical orientations and methods are being developed in anthropology (Ortner, 1984, p. 127).

We also need to recognize from the start that the definition of *practices* inevitably raises questions for developmental psychologists about the difference between *practices* and *activities*. That issue is taken up by Michael Cole in his chapter. At this point, however, we shall note that most scholars who use the term *practices* do so without a knowledge of the terms *activities, activity theory,* or *activity system.* These terms are the province of psychologists. Psychologists interested in *activity theory* also make use of the term *practices,* however. The Laboratory of Comparative Human Cognition, for instance, uses both terms, drawing from Lave's (1988) analysis of "cognition in practice" and from Scribner and Cole's (1981) definition of practice as "a recurrent goal-directed sequence of activities using a particular technology and particular systems of knowledge" (p. 235). Writing, in this definition, may be an activity. Literacy practices, however, cover the specific ways in which writing is used: its implements, how it is understood, and the specific purposes it is used for in everyday life.

Reconciling definitions could become a major enterprise in itself, and we have let Michael Cole take the lead on that task. With an eye to the question, What would you do with the concept of practice? we have adopted a working definition that combines features from several disciplines and theoretical perspectives.

Our definition starts by noting that practices are actions. The term *practices* refers to what people do—that is, to matters that are open to observation by the researcher and by others in a social group. Thus, one of the appeals of attention to practices lies in their observability. However, what is open to observation is not behavior in the behaviorist sense but rather meaningful action, action that is situated in a context and open to interpretation.

Of course, by this minimal criterion, all human actions would count as practices (Ortner, 1984). The definition that we have found most useful adds several qualifiers. It emphasizes actions that have a routine or repeated quality to them. To use Scribner and Cole's definition, practice is "a *recurrent* . . . sequence of activities" (emphasis added). Our definition also adds the qualifiers "social" or "cultural." These terms point to actions that are engaged in by many or most members of a cultural group and that carry with them normative expectations about how things should be done (Laboratory of Comparative Human Cognition, 1983). Cultural practices are not neutral; they come packaged with values about what is natural, mature, morally right, or aesthetically pleasing. These, then, are actions that may easily become part of a group's identity. As people learn the practice—its essential and optional features—they also develop values and a sense of belonging and identity within the community (Holland and Valsiner, 1988; Lave and Wenger, 1991). At the same time, the shared quality of the practice means that it may be sustained, changed, or challenged by a variety of people.

In sum, practices are actions that are repeated, shared with others in a social group, and invested with normative expectations and with meanings or significances that go beyond the immediate goals of the action.

Why Would Developmentalists Be Interested in Such a Concept?

Among developmentalists, an interest in practices stems from the recognition that human development occurs in cultural contexts and from the sense that models that integrate the cultural with the developmental, and that can be implemented in research, are still not readily at hand. The notion of cultural practices has come to appeal as a construct that will both contextualize development and provide a way of bringing together what are often described under the separate labels of thinking, doing, feeling, and becoming. These points will be discussed more fully below. Still another source of interest stems from the challenge that accounts of practices often offer to the way we think about development.

Bourdieu's analysis of practices will provide an example (Bourdieu, 1977, 1990). Bourdieu is a key figure within anthropological descriptions of practices. To start with, he offers an account of the end-state of development that is different from what one finds in current conceptions of development, including Vygotsky's (1978). Those accounts present development as moving toward action that is increasingly goal-directed and likely to be reflected upon. Bourdieu reminds us that most social behavior is habitual and automatic. As practices get repeated again and again, they come to be seen as part of a "natural" order, with the original reasons for their occurrence difficult to resurrect.

In a further challenge to what we may perceive as the outcome of development, Bourdieu emphasizes the impact of a practice upon relationships (rather than upon the skill or knowledge of an individual) and upon relationships characterized in terms other than differences in expertise (the usual emphasis in many analyses of learning). In Bourdieu's analysis, participants are ideologically positioned relative to one another and seek to protect their interests. When power and status are asymmetrically distributed, as in teacher-pupil and parent-child relationships, the less powerful party's access to resources—definition of tasks, rights to talk, control of conceptual tools—is limited. The implication for development is that the world that children move through may need to be seen as forceful and demanding, not "free market and benign" as many cognitive developmental theories assume (Goodnow, 1990).

We have taken Bourdieu as a single source. In his chapter, Michael Cole brings out additional intellectual antecedents that have sparked the interest of developmentalists. Rather than explore these at this point, however, we move to the set of propositions that frame this volume (propositions adapted from Goodnow, 1993).

Conceptual Framework for the Volume

We shall describe each proposition in general terms and ground it in studies of language—a grounding that offers a first indication of how the concept of practice has been translated into research. We begin with a general proposition that applies to all the chapters within this volume and then move to the propositions that gave rise to our selecting particular research.

PROPOSITION 1: *Practices provide a way of describing development-in-context, without separating child and context and without separating development into a variety of separate domains.*

This baseline proposition addresses several interrelated concerns that have arisen in developmental psychology. The first is to move beyond the individual considered in isolation, to make a place for the social/cultural/historical context. The second is to move beyond the passive individual shaped by socializing agents, to make room for the active, constructive, transforming, (or resisting) person. What is sought is an understanding of society and individuals that avoids the twin hazards of "individual constructivism" and "social determinism." The one emphasizes the individual to such an extent that minimal attention is given to the way objects are socially defined, actions are socially constrained, and the acquisition of some forms of knowledge is promoted and of others is restricted or prohibited. The other sees the social context as shaping the individual to such an extent that attention to choice, resistance, or intention becomes minimal.

Both of these extremes are avoided when the person-participating-in-a-practice is taken as the unit of analysis. This approach treats individual and context as interdependent and mutually active. Context is not conceptualized as separate from the person, nor is the relationship between individual and society conceived in X-on-Y terms—that is, in terms of the effect of society upon people, of people upon society, or of context upon development. Instead, individuals and society are seen as mutually constituted or co-created. Society produces persons of a particular kind and at the same time people produce society.

This approach implies a much more dynamic conception of context than is commonly assumed. Contexts are treated not as static givens, dictated by the social and physical environment, but as ongoing accomplishments negotiated by participants. In the study of discourse, this shift from static to dynamic is signaled by the use of such terms as *contextualization* and *recontextualization*—a move that focuses attention on the process by which participants themselves determine which aspects of the ongoing activity are relevant (Bauman and C. Briggs, 1990; Ochs, 1990). A cultural practices approach to development thus offers a holistic conception of individual and context as an interlocking system in which the practices change along with the person (see Rogoff, Baker-Sennett, Lacasa, and Goldsmith, this volume).

This approach is holistic in another way as well. It addresses a third concern that has arisen in developmental psychology, a concern to break down the segregation of thinking from other parts of life—the separation of thinking from what we call "doing" or "being," the division between "cognitive" development, on the one hand, and "social," "emotional," or "personal" development on the other. In contrast to this separation, the concept of *practice* recognizes that the acquisition of knowledge or skill is part of the construction of an identity or a person.

This point is exemplified in research that takes a practice perspective on narrative. By studying everyday discourse in families and communities, researchers have discovered that young children from a variety of sociocultural groups participate routinely in personal storytelling by two to three years of age. (See, for example, Sperry and Sperry, 1991; Miller, Fung, and Mintz, in press; Miller and Sperry, 1988.) Here is a practice—telling stories about one's past experiences—that transcends any single developmental "domain." It is obviously relevant to cognitive and linguistic development, for it involves re-creating in the here and now events that happened at some previous time. It is also a social phenomenon: often the past experiences are social experiences, and the activity of narrating those experiences is a social activity, involving narrators, listeners, and other participants. At the same time, personal storytelling belongs to the domain of self and identity. When people narrate remembered experiences from their own lives, they are expressing who they are. Being self-referential, these stories are unlikely to be neutral; they are bound up with the narrator's evaluation or affective stance toward the past experience and with the moral values and frameworks by which experience is interpreted, ordered, and assessed. Personal storytelling is thus also relevant to emotional and moral development. When the object of study is the child-participating-in-story-telling, it becomes possible to keep the whole child in view and to see that narrators and listeners are engaged as acting, thinking, feeling, valuing persons.

PROPOSITION 2: *Practices reflect or instantiate a social and moral order.*

From this perspective, development may be regarded as a process of coming to interpret, understand, and perhaps accept the principles that this order contains. This proposition is at the core of Chapter Two (by Richard Shweder, Lene Arnett Jensen, and William Goldstein), on sleeping arrangements in two cultures. It is as well a proposition with echoes from many quarters. In Ortner's terms, "Much of system reproduction takes place via the routinized activities and intimate interactions of domestic life" (Ortner, 1984, p. 156).

A major issue that arises in connection with this proposition is that the meaning of a practice is not transparent (Packer, 1987). How, then, can researchers derive the system from the practice? One response to this question is based on reports of practices solicited from participants. Practices often provide an easier basis for reporting than beliefs or values do. That is, I can tell you what I do and what I would find acceptable, and you can use that report as a base for exploring what the behavior means to me. This approach is exemplified in the chapter by Shweder and his colleagues, a chapter concerned with ways to isolate the principles involved in sleeping arrangements.

The techniques described in that chapter have their parallels in studies of language socialization. Recordings of discourse practices have been used, for example, to collect after-the-fact interpretations and cross-validations from the participants (Schieffelin, 1990).

Language studies have also contributed several other techniques that are adaptable to a variety of content areas. One way to "read" practices is to ground the researcher's interpretation of the meaning of a practice in observations (or participant-observations) of the practices themselves. The researcher makes audio- or video-recorded observations of children in the contexts of everyday life and then conducts micro-level analyses of particular types of routine discursive events, paying attention not only to the semantic content of what is said but to the form and function of discourse. The researcher follows in the tracks of the discourse, exploiting the same public cues—for example, repetition of key words, tone of voice, pointed silences, explicit morals, laughter—that participants themselves use when they interpret one another's behavior "on-line" (see Bauman and C. Briggs, 1990; Garvey, 1992; Schieffelin and Ochs, 1986).

Characteristic features that recur across instances of a type of discourse will point to other discourse types that are relevant to interpreting the first. For example, the finding that personal storytelling was used by Chinese caregivers to shame young children led to the discovery of a related class of shaming events in which caregivers used other shaming techniques (Fung, 1994).

Another resource in everyday discourse that has been exploited by observers attempting to understand the meaning of practices is children's inevitable departures from adult standards and the ensuing "corrections," explanations, and instructions from caregivers, older siblings, or teachers (Much and Shweder, 1978). These naturally occurring errors and repairs make tacit assumptions available to participants and observers. Ethnographers have also examined their own inadvertent violations of the local ways of speaking as a source of evidence about the cultural principles expressed in talk (for example, C. Briggs, 1986).

By these several methods—reports of practices, observations of practices, or a combination of both—researchers explore not only the meanings that practices hold for people but also the degree of their commitment to or investment in them.

PROPOSITION 3: *Practices provide the route by which children come to participate in a culture, allowing the culture to be "reproduced" or "transformed."*

Development may be regarded as a change in the nature of participation in a practice. Chapter Three (by Barbara Rogoff, Jacqueline Baker-Sennett, Pilar Lacasa, and Denise Goldsmith), which studies Girl Scout cookie sales, rests on this proposition. The seemingly simple idea that children participate with others in cultural practices implies a much more complex relationship between children and culture than is commonly assumed.

Often children are regarded as the temporary "have-nots" of culture; they enter the world innocent of culture, with adulthood as their destination. This view is tacit in the term "acquisition of culture" and in traditional understandings of childhood socialization and development. A conception of development as change in participation challenges this view as too narrow without denying that child participants may get better at doing things or develop understandings that resemble those of more experienced members of their culture.

Let us elaborate first on the latter point and then turn to the challenges. It is common in research on practices to find descriptions of children who are becoming more fluent, more skilled, or more responsible participants. Indeed, for those who study young children, a chief advantage of a practice perspective is that it makes it possible to trace such developments from their earliest roots. For example, by attending to the verbal and nonverbal ways in which youngsters participate in events of narration, one can study narrative development in children long before they are able to fully comprehend others' stories, tell their own stories without assistance, or give a name—"telling stories"—to what they are doing. By taking this approach, researchers have found that in some cultural groups the parent or other more experienced participant structures the task of co-narration and gradually hands over to the child more and more responsibility for telling the story (Fivush, 1993). In addition to narrative skills, it has been proposed that autobiographical memory (Nelson, 1993) and gender-appropriate emotional expression (Fivush, 1993) develop through participation in scaffolded co-narrations of this sort.

However, the notion of development as change in participation also implies that children may participate with their companions in ways that are not necessarily "progressive." Certain styles of parental co-narration may actually impede fuller participation (McCabe and Peterson, 1991). In her research on "sharing time" in kindergarten classrooms, Michaels (1991) describes the "dismantling" of minority children's storytelling. This happens when teacher and child operate with different, ethnically correlated narrative styles and are unable to negotiate meaningful collaborations.

In addition to challenging our assumptions about the direction of change, this proposition has prompted researchers to look beyond a single form of participation—often one that is standard in one's own cultural group—to the variety of ways in which cultures structure children's everyday participation in cultural practices. Again turning to studies of narrative by way of illustration, we see that the role of co-narrator in scaffolded interactions is only one of many participant roles to which children have access (Goodwin, 1990; Miller and others, 1990; Ochs and Taylor, 1992). Instead of being offered slots in a co-narration, children may have to come up with a clever narrative in order to get the floor (Heath, 1983). And individuals may need to be alert to stories "aimed" at or intended for them (Basso, 1984).

These multiple forms of participation not only imply plural developmental pathways but point to the many ways in which children contribute to the production of culture. Despite the relative powerlessness of children, their participation is crucial to the maintenance and reproduction of a culture's language practices. In effect, studies of language repeat a basic theme found in the chapter by Rogoff, Baker-Sennett, Lacasa, and Goldsmith. Their analysis shows that the community-wide practice of Girl Scout cookie sales changes along with individual girls' participation in the practice. Children re-create culture as they learn to participate in the practice. This is a most significant challenge to traditional views of the relationship between children and culture.

PROPOSITION 4: *Practices do not exist in isolation.*

Each practice has a history and is part of other practices that may offer supporting or competing alternatives. Development may be regarded as a process of learning about options, limits, and blends that are acceptable to oneself or to others. This proposition is central to Chapter Four, Barbara Miller's chapter on the dress and hair practices of second-generation Hindu Indian immigrants in the United States. She examines the choices—including creative combinations of practices—that these adolescents make in the face of conflicts between the traditional Hindu culture of their parents and the "popular culture" of their peers.

In addition to immigration, another situation in which competing cultural practices are highly visible is societies that are undergoing rapid social change—a situation that affects a large number of the world's children. Traditional practices may be transformed or even replaced from one generation to the next (Heath, 1990). Or, less dramatically, people may add new justifications for old practices. For example, Shaw (1994) reports that young people in Taiwan are beginning to justify the traditional practice of caring for the older generation by reference not only to the Confucian ideal of "filial piety" but to the "modern" values of reciprocity and egalitarianism. The relationship between practices and justifications may also shift in the opposite direction as old principles are extended to justify changes in practices (Goodnow and Bowes, 1994).

It would be misleading, however, to imply that multiple practices exist only in the "special" cases of immigration or rapid social change. In fact, every culture—even small-scale traditional cultures (J. Briggs, 1992)—has more than one view of the world, more than one way of doing things. Descriptions have taken many forms. For example, Gramsci (1971) describes dominant ideologies as "hegemonic," dubbing competing ideologies as "counter-hegemonic." D'Andrade and Strauss (1992) describe "cultural models" as essentially "multiple" and "contested." That is, models actively compete with one another rather than placidly co-exist. (The double quality of "multiple" and "contested" is the essence of what is often referred to as "pluralism" rather than "multiplicity.")

Although diversity of perspectives is a fact of cultural life, it is important to emphasize that people are not necessarily granted the right to choose among perspectives. This is a lesson that many children have to learn when they enter school. They may be expected to speak a language or dialect that differs from their own or use forms of discourse that violate community standards (for example, Philips, 1972). Conversely, valued ways of using language may be unacceptable in the classroom (for example, Michaels, 1991).

Whether the message is that one does not have a choice or that one's choices consist of this or that set of alternatives, what is at stake, as Miller's chapter shows, are issues of identity, both for the individual and for the immigrant community. This point harks back to the inseparability of individual and community development that we saw in the study by Rogoff and her colleagues and anticipates our final proposition.

PROPOSITION 5: *The nature of participation has consequences.*

These consequences are sometimes limited to the particular situations in which participation occurs and sometimes extend beyond them. Development may be regarded, then, as the tightening or the recontextualization of situation-bound understandings. This proposition has been explored predominantly with reference to consequences in the form of the way we understand a task or use a strategy. Tasks and strategies that involve arithmetic practices have been favored as a research base, in part because arithmetic practices bring out with particular clarity the ways in which different situations—the street, the classroom, the supermarket, the kitchen—alter the ways in which arithmetic is used and understood.

Chapter Five, by Terezinha Nunes, capitalizes on this rewarding base. It has as well, however, the advantage of bringing out a consequence that seldom appears in studies of arithmetic practices: a consequence for a person's sense of identity—a person's sense, for instance, of him- or herself as a "practical" or a "schooled" person. That sense of identity arises from the practices and then feeds back into the choice of particular arithmetic procedures.

How is any sense of identity, any sense of self, constructed in the course of practices? And how may we best observe the process of construction? Those questions have only begun to surface within studies of number practices. Studies of language, however, suggest that the best place to turn is to everyday discourse—to what is sometimes called "speaking praxis." The processes of self-construction, it is argued, are best observed by considering discourse (narrative especially) rather than by using such units of analysis as the word or the sentence (see, for example, Bruner, 1990; Nelson, 1989; Miller and others, 1992). A discourse approach leads to the proposal that selves are continually created and re-created through the child's participation in narrative discourse—a view that contrasts with two common views: that language is merely a window into the self and that its role is limited to enabling one to think about oneself as an object.

We have used the term *selves* in the preceding sentence: deliberately so. There is, in fact, an interesting parallel between Nunes's arguments against the notion of "ability" and current concerns about the concept of the "self." The implication of ability as a steady state, Nunes points out, is not in keeping with the fact that we can often solve a problem when it is presented in one way or one situation but not in another. In similar fashion, the implication of the self as a fixed quality of the individual is not in keeping with proposals grounded in discourse practices—proposals that stress the dynamic, multiple, and variable quality of selves (Miller and others, 1990, 1992).

Along with consequences related to cognitive strategies and situated selves, we would draw attention to the motivational and affective consequences of participation in practices. It needs to be said at the outset that the number of developmental studies that have taken a cultural practices approach to affect is small compared to those that have focused on cognition. This may reflect, in part, the fact that the motivational and affective side of practice is relatively undeveloped in practice theories (Ortner, 1984).

Several kinds of affective consequences of participation in everyday discourse can be identified. One is the formation of emotional bonds between people. In her research with the Kaluli of Papua, New Guinea, Schieffelin (1990) describes how affectively charged relationships between younger brothers and older sisters are created through routine participation in a type of interaction in which brothers appeal for help and sisters respond with nurturance. This example also points to another consequence: the creation of particular feelings. In this case, girls are supposed to "feel sorry" or "have pity" for their brothers, and mothers "coach" this feeling by using a distinctive voice quality.

A further kind of affective consequence brings us back to the unity of thinking, feeling, acting, and becoming: children may develop emotionally differentiated understandings of which lessons are especially important to learn. "Shaping the mind," as practiced by the Kwara'ae of the Solomon Islands, provides an excellent example (Watson-Gegeo, 1992). This "affectively intense and symbolically powerful" discourse is used to remind targeted individuals of key cultural values and to restore proper conduct and interpersonal harmony (Watson-Gegeo, 1992, p. 62).

We might also think of "shaping the mind"—and all the other practices that we have referred to in this chapter—in terms of emotional investment. Because practices recur in everyday life, they provide participants with repeated opportunities to invest in values, in ways of interpreting experience, and in the practice itself. Here, too, participation leaves its mark on the person through the production of affective stance: enthusiastic involvement, indifference, resistance, playfulness. And, like ability and identity, affective stance is likely to get created and re-created in practice.

The presence of consequences is the last of the propositions that we constructed to cut across a variety of studies and provide a framework for this volume. With these outlined, and with some reasons for developmentalists' interest in the concept of practices laid out, let us turn to the more specific chapters.

References

Basso, K. H. "'Stalking with Stories': Names, Places, and Moral Narratives Among the Western Apache." In E. M. Bruner and S. Plattner (eds.), *Text, Play, and Story: The Construction and Reconstruction of Self and Society*. Washington, D.C.: American Ethnological Society, 1984.

Bauman, R., and Briggs, C. L. "Poetics and Performance as Critical Perspectives on Language and Social Life." *Annual Review of Anthropology*, 1990, *19*, 59–88.

Bourdieu, P. *Outline of a Theory of Practice*. New York: Cambridge University Press, 1977.

Bourdieu, P. *The Logic of Practice*. Palo Alto, Calif.: Stanford University Press, 1990.

Briggs, C. L. *Learning How to Ask: A Sociolinguistic Appraisal of the Role of the Interview in Social Science Research*. New York: Cambridge University Press, 1986.

Briggs, J. L. "Mazes of Meaning: How a Child and a Culture Create Each Other." In W. A. Corsaro and P. J. Miller (eds.), *Interpretive Approaches to Children's Socialization*. New Directions for Child Development, no. 58. San Francisco: Jossey-Bass, 1992.

Bruner, J. *Acts of Meaning*. Cambridge, Mass.: Harvard University Press, 1990.

D'Andrade, R. G., and Strauss, C. *Human Motives and Cultural Models*. New York: Cambridge University Press, 1992.

Fivush, R. "Emotional Content of Parent-Child Conversations About the Past." In C. A. Nelson (ed.), *Memory and Affect in Development*. Minnesota Symposia on Child Psychology, no. 26. Hillsdale, N.J.: Erlbaum, 1993.

Fung, H. "The Socialization of Shame in Young Chinese Children." Unpublished doctoral dissertation, Department of Psychology, University of Chicago, 1994.

Garvey, C. (ed.). "Talk in the Study of Socialization and Development" (special issue). *Merrill-Palmer Quarterly*, 1992, *38*.

Goodnow, J. J. "The Socialization of Cognition: What's Involved?" In J. W. Stigler, R. A. Shweder, and G. Herdt (eds.), *Cultural Psychology: Essays on Comparative Human Development*. New York: Cambridge University Press, 1990.

Goodnow, J. J. "Cultural Practices: Contributions and Questions from the Study of Household Tasks." Paper presented at the biennial meeting of the Society for Research in Child Development, New Orleans, Mar. 27, 1993.

Goodnow, J. J., and Bowes, J. A. *Men, Women, and Household Work: New Ways for Old*. New York: Oxford University Press, 1994.

Goodwin, M. H. *He-Said-She-Said: Talk as Social Organization Among Black Children*. Bloomington: Indiana University Press, 1990.

Gramsci, A. *Selections from the Prison Notebooks*. London: Lawrence & Wishart, 1971.

Heath, S. B. *Ways with Words: Language, Life, and Work in Communities and Classrooms*. New York: Cambridge University Press, 1983.

Heath, S. B. "The Children of Trackton's Children: Spoken and Written Language in Social Change." In J. W. Stigler, R. A. Shweder, and G. Herdt (eds.), *Cultural Psychology: Essays on Comparative Human Development*. New York: Cambridge University Press, 1990.

Holland, D. C., and Valsiner, J. "Cognition, Symbols, and Vygotsky's Developmental Psychology," *Ethos*, 1988, *16*, 247–272.

Laboratory of Comparative Human Cognition. "Culture and Cognitive Development." In W. Kessen (ed.), *Mussen's Handbook of Child Psychology*. Vol. 1. (4th ed.) New York: Wiley, 1983.

Lave, J. *Cognition in Practice: Mind, Mathematics, and Culture in Everyday Life*. New York: Cambridge University Press, 1988.

Lave, J., and Wenger, E. *Situated Learning: Legitimate Peripheral Participation*. New York: Cambridge University Press, 1991.

McCabe, A., and Peterson, C. "Getting the Story: A Longitudinal Study of Parental Styles in Eliciting Narratives and Developing Narrative Skill." In A. McCabe and C. Peterson (eds.), *Developing Narrative Structure*. Hillsdale, N.J.: Erlbaum, 1991.

Michaels, S. "The Dismantling of Narrative." In A. McCabe and C. Peterson (eds.), *Developing Narrative Structure*. Hillsdale, N.J.: Erlbaum, 1991.

Miller, P. J., Fung, H., and Mintz, J. "Self-Construction Through Narrative Practices: A Chinese and American Comparison of Early Socialization." *Ethos*, in press.

Miller, P. J., and Sperry, L. L. "Early Talk About the Past: The Origins of Conversational Stories of Personal Experience." *Journal of Child Language*, 1988, *15*, 293–315.

Miller, P. J., and others. "Narrative Practices and the Social Construction of Self in Childhood." *American Ethnologist*, 1990, *17*, 292–311.

Miller, P. J., and others. "The Narrated Self: Young Children's Construction of Self in Relation to Others in Conversational Stories of Personal Experience." *Merrill-Palmer Quarterly*, 1992, *38*, 45–67.

Much, N., and Shweder, R. A. "Speaking of Rules: The Analysis of Culture in the Breach." In W. Damon (ed.), *Moral Development*. New Directions for Child Development, no. 2. San Francisco: Jossey-Bass, 1978.

Nelson, K. (ed.). *Narratives from the Crib*. Cambridge, Mass.: Harvard University Press, 1989.

Nelson, K. "The Psychological and Social Origins of Autobiographical Memory." *Psychological Science*, 1993, *4*, 7–14.

Ochs, E. "Indexicality and Socialization." In J. W. Stigler, R. A. Shweder, and G. Herdt (eds.), *Cultural Psychology: Essays on Comparative Human Development*. New York: Cambridge University Press, 1990.

Ochs, E., and Taylor, C. "Family Narrative as Political Activity." *Discourse and Society*, 1992, *3*, 301–340.

Ortner, S. "Theory in Anthropology Since the Sixties." *Society for Comparative Study of Society and History*, 1984, *26*, 126–166.

Packer, M. J. "Social Interaction as Practical Activity: Implications for the Study of Social and Moral Development." In W. Kurtines and J. Gewirtz (eds.), *Moral Development Through Social Interaction*. New York: Wiley, 1987.

Philips, S. U. "Participant Structures and Communicative Competence: Warm Springs Children in Community and Classroom." In C. B. Cazden, V. P. John, and D. Hymes (eds.), *Functions of Language in the Classroom*. New York: Teachers College Press, 1972.

Schieffelin, B. B. *The Give and Take of Everyday Life: Language Socialization of Kaluli Children*. New York: Cambridge University Press, 1990.

Schieffelin, B. B., and Ochs, E. (eds.). *Language Socialization Across Cultures*. New York: Cambridge University Press, 1986.

Scribner, S., and Cole, M. *The Psychology of Literacy*. Cambridge, Mass.: Harvard University Press, 1981.

Shaw, T. A. "Modernity's New Sources of Self." Paper presented at a meeting of the Society for Cross-Cultural Research, Santa Fe, N.Mex., Feb. 20, 1994.

Sperry, L. L., and Sperry, D. E. "The Socialization of Narration in African-American Toddlers." Paper presented at the biennial meeting of the Society for Research in Child Development, Apr. 1991.

Vygotsky, L. S. *Mind in Society: The Development of Higher Psychological Processes*. Cambridge, Mass.: Harvard University Press, 1978.

Watson-Gegeo, K. A. "Thick Explanation in the Ethnographic Study of Child Socialization: A Longitudinal Study of the Problem of Schooling for Kwara'ae (Solomon Island) Children." In W. A. Cosaro and P. J. Miller (eds.), *Interpretive Approaches to Children's Socialization*. New Directions for Child Development, no. 58. San Francisco: Jossey-Bass, 1992.

PEGGY J. MILLER *is associate professor, Department of Speech Communication and Department of Psychology, University of Illinois, Urbana-Champaign.*

JACQUELINE J. GOODNOW *is professorial research fellow, School of Behavioral Sciences, Macquarie University, Sydney.*

Editors' Preface to
"Who Sleeps by Whom Revisited"

Once the decision is made to explore practices, several questions rapidly come into play. Which practices shall I work with? Shall I concentrate upon observations or go beyond that to ask for comment? Shall I ask for comment upon the practices followed or upon those not followed? On what grounds shall I make such decisions? These several questions are taken up in the following chapter by Richard Shweder, Lene Arnett Jensen, and William Goldstein—a study that is one of several in which Shweder has pursued an interest in cultural definitions of moral issues.

The study explores a specific family practice: Which family members share a bed or sleeping space? As a content area for research, the practice of sleeping arrangements is marked by several interesting features. First, it evokes strong feelings as to what is right, wrong, or even pathological. The choice of practice clearly fits Ortner's (1984) advice that the practices most likely to provide rewarding research topics are those that have strong affect attached to them: a strong sense of either their propriety or their "wrongness."

Second, what is regarded both as right and as wrong varies across cultures. To take an example from Shweder and his colleagues, many people outside North America regard as cruel the practice, widespread in North America, of isolating the young child from the parental bed.

Third, there is the promise of being able to pursue the argument that the description of a context or a culture needs to go beyond the description of practices and ask, What are the meanings of the practice to the people involved? Sleeping arrangements exemplify particularly well a methodological challenge. Because the practice tends to be taken for granted, people are likely to find it harder to talk about why family members sleep where they do than to talk about why it is important to read regularly to young children or to childproof the house when an infant starts to walk. Shweder and his colleagues address this issue not only by asking what other possibilities logically exist (and which of these are represented in the actual practices) but also by asking informants to rank various possible arrangements according to the extent to which they are morally offensive.

In these prefatory remarks, we seek to give both a sense of the chapter that follows and a sense of its background. The broadest background in this case is a general concern with the ways in which practices and principles are interrelated (a concern reminiscent of psychologists' debates about degrees of correspondence between actions and attitudes).

Part of that concern is the recognition that there is not likely to be any neat one-to-one correspondence: one practice, one principle. As we noted in Chapter One, the reasons are several. A variety of practices may meet the same principle, and practices that appear similar at the behavioral level may stem from different principles. (Both of these points are well made by Shweder, Jensen, and Goldstein in their chapter.) In addition, a single action may be designed to "piggyback" several concerns (Goodnow, 1988) or may combine yesterday's valid reasons with the inertia of custom (LeVine, 1988).

Procedurally, that conceptual recognition leads research in several directions. First, it tends to amalgamate a number of actions: putting together, say, a parent's disciplinary actions over a series of occasions and relating these, rather than a single action, to some underlying principle (as in Kochanska, Kuczynski, and Radke-Yarrow, 1989). The amalgamation, it is proposed, wipes out some of the day-to-day variations, leaving as one's data the common ground, the core that is most likely to be related to principles. The procedure prompts the questions: When is a practice likely to vary from one occasion to another? What parts of a practice are most (or least) likely to vary?

A second research direction consists of accepting the presence of multiple principles or moral concerns and moving to the question, What are these, and how are they interrelated? Shweder and his colleagues, for instance, isolate four concerns that the Oriya in India bring to sleeping arrangements: concerns with incest (brothers and sisters over a certain age are separated), with protecting the vulnerable young child (there is always a parent nearby), with preserving the chastity and public image of young women (no daughter over a certain age sleeps unchaperoned), and with status (the higher the status, the more solo the space). The kind of interrelationship they propose for these four is in the form of a hierarchy of concerns. Avoiding incest, for instance, has priority over the other three concerns; status gives way to the other three.

Shweder and his colleagues are not alone in their interest in the internal structure of various rules or schemas, of course. That approach is also to be found, for instance, in Mancuso and Lehrer's (1986) proposals for hierarchies in the rules regulating the way members of a family should treat one another. It is also to be found in analyses of the extent to which various ideas or principles form clusters, sometimes logically consistent with one another, sometimes not (for example, Goodnow and Warton, 1992; Mugny and Carugati, 1989; Palacios, 1990). In all these cases, the concern is with locating an "internal structure," with specifying the ways in which the several concerns that feed into practices are related to one another.

The background of interest in practices and principles contains as well the conceptual recognition that there is not always a neat correspondence between what people give as the reasons for what they do and what observers see as the reasons. The bases proposed for this lack of correspondence are again several. Informants may be able to describe the principles involved only in vague terms. "We're a family," for instance, is the response that Goodnow and Delaney (1989) were often given when they asked Australian mothers why they expected children to do household jobs. Informants may not have words at all for what they take so much for granted. (Wittgenstein, in fact, argued that the most significant concerns are the ones least verbalized.) The lack of correspondence is especially likely to be the case, in Bourdieu's view, when a motive needs to be disguised: when, for instance, self-interest needs to be hidden because it threatens the image of a group whose members have some minimal interest in not savaging each other (Bourdieu, 1990).

Procedurally, what does this conceptual recognition lead to? The chapter by Shweder and his colleagues illustrates an approach for which Garfinkel (1967) has become especially well known: propose a practice that violates the principles you suspect are involved and then ask for comment. How offensive to you would this kind of sleeping arrangement be? As Garfinkel points out, people are often better able to tell you what is "out of the question" than what is possible; the violations often prompt a clearer statement of principle. In addition, the researcher has the opportunity to check possibilities that have not been spontaneously verbalized at all by the informant but that represent the researcher's sense of what underlies a practice.

Two last comments need to be made before we turn to the chapter itself. First, it is often said that the way in which a principle is played out in practice is influenced by the specific circumstances of a particular time and place. That kind of general statement is easy to make. Checking it or concretizing it calls for some ingenuity, however: all the more reason to note the way Shweder and his colleagues have pinned down "circumstances" in terms of the particular resources represented by the number of rooms available in a house. In a later chapter, Barbara Rogoff and her colleagues translate "resources" into the order forms that Girl Scouts have available for recording orders for cookies. The implementation is different in the two cases, but the intent is the same: to find a way of demonstrating the impact of what is available at a particular time upon the way a principle is played out.

Our final comment has to do with the fact that this chapter on sleeping arrangements is an opening chapter in two ways: in the sense of being the first of the set and in the sense of raising questions that will be picked up again in the later chapters, questions, for example, about the variability of practices (across occasions and among members of a social group) and about the interrelationship of practices and the principles underlying them. There is, however, one major difference between this opening chapter and the others in the set. Developmental questions are not in the foreground of the paper on sleeping arrangements. Instead, the chapter covers adults' accounts of possible and impossible arrangements, using these as a way to articulate the principles that adults follow and that children may abstract and adopt in whole or in part. The next step is to ask, What does this kind of approach lead us to explore when it comes to children's viewpoints? Do children acquire some principles before others? How and when do they acquire a sense of the possible and the impossible? How and when do they acquire not only an awareness of the proper practices but also of the moral affect that goes with the sense of possible/impossible? These developmental questions are worth keeping in mind throughout the remaining chapters.

References

Bourdieu, P. *The Logic of Practice.* Palo Alto, Calif.: Stanford University Press, 1990.

Garfinkel, H. *Studies in Ethnomethodology.* Englewood Cliffs, N.J.: Prentice Hall, 1967.

Goodnow, J. J. "Parents' Ideas, Actions, and Feelings: Models and Methods from Developmental and Social Psychology." *Child Development,* 1988, *59,* 286–320.

Goodnow, J. J., and Delaney, S. "Children's Household Work: Differentiating Types of Work and Styles of Assignment." *Journal of Applied Developmental Psychology,* 1989, *10,* 209–226.

Goodnow, J. J., and Warton, P. M. "Contexts and Cognitions: Taking a Pluralist View." In P. Light and G. Butterworth (eds.), *Context and Cognition.* London: Harvester Wheatsheaf, 1992.

Kochanska, G., Kuczynski, L., and Radke-Yarrow, M. "Correspondence Between Mothers' Self-Reported and Observed Child-Rearing Practices." *Child Development,* 1989, *61,* 138–151.

LeVine, R. A. "Human Parental Care: Universal Goals, Cultural Strategies, Individual Behavior." In R. A. LeVine, P. M. Miller, and M. M. West (eds.), *Parental Behavior in Diverse Societies.* New Directions for Child Development, no. 40. San Francisco: Jossey-Bass, 1988.

Mancuso, J. C., and Lehrer, R. "Cognitive Processes During Reactions to Rule Violation." In R. D. Ashmore and D. M. Brodzinsky (eds.), *Thinking About the Family: Views of Parents and Children.* Hillsdale, N.J.: Erlbaum, 1986.

Mugny, G., and Carugati, F. *Social Representations of Intelligence.* New York: Cambridge University Press, 1989.

Ortner, S. "Theory in Anthropology Since the Sixties." *Comparative Studies in Society and History,* 1984, *26,* 126–166.

Palacios, J. "Parents' Ideas About the Development and Education of Their Children: Answers to Some Questions." *International Journal of Behavioral Development,* 1990, *13,* 137–155.

The practice of determining who sleeps by whom in a family household is a symbolic action that simultaneously expresses and realizes some of the deepest moral ideals of a cultural community.

Who Sleeps by Whom Revisited: A Method for Extracting the Moral Goods Implicit in Practice

Richard A. Shweder, Lene Arnett Jensen, William M. Goldstein

The focus of this chapter is on the analysis of sleeping arrangements among high-caste families in the Hindu temple town of Bhubaneswar in Orissa, India, and among middle-class families from the Anglo-American culture region of Hyde Park, Chicago. Our central claim is that the universal practice of determining "who sleeps by whom" in a family household is a symbolic action, or nonverbal vehicle of meaning, that both expresses and realizes some of the deepest moral ideals of a cultural community. One aim of the chapter is to discuss methods for extracting the preferences, values, or moral "goods" implicit in the practice of arranging where family members sleep at night. A second aim is to make a substantive contribution to cultural psychology by tracing some interconnections between cultural practices, morality, ethnopsychological knowledge, and personality development.

We begin, however, with a discussion of a recent commentary by the renowned pediatrician T. Berry Brazelton on the topic of parent-child co-sleeping arrangements (Brazelton, 1990). Brazelton's didactic, self-conscious rumination

We gratefully acknowledge the support received for this research from the National Institute of Child Health and Human Development and the MacArthur Foundation Research Network on Successful Midlife Development (MIDMAC). We are deeply thankful to Manamohan Mahapatra for his many contributions over the years to our research in Orissa, India, and thankful as well to Joan Miller, Chita Mohanty, Swapna Pani, and Candy Shweder for their assistance in connection with the gathering and early analysis of some of the material on sleeping arrangements in Orissa.

ponders the question, Who *ought* to sleep by whom in the human family? His candid reflections, although brief, are deep and revealing. They provide students of cultural psychology and Anglo-American cultural studies with a glimpse of the way ethnopediatric "wisdom," local moral sensibilities, culture-specific character traits, and historically evolved family practices reinforce each other—and perhaps even make each other up.

Brazelton's Conflict

Brazelton poses a fascinating and complex moral question: Should children be allowed (encouraged, required) routinely to sleep in the same bed with their parent(s)? For most middle-class readers who have grown up in the Anglo-American culture region, the answer to that question will seem obvious: children should be taught to sleep alone.

In the past, that was the answer Brazelton would have given to parents. More recently, however, he has had some conversations with pediatricians in Japan, where children typically co-sleep with their parents until they are adolescents. Now he feels "conflicted." On the one hand, Brazelton believes it is important to promote autonomy and independence in infants and young children by having them sleep alone. He also worries about the temptations and dangers of sexual abuse; and he cannot shake from his mind the picture of the sexual fantasy life of young children (desiring the mother, hating the father, dreading genital mutilation) as portrayed by psychoanalytic theorists. He even acknowledges his own inhibitions and his inability to sleep in the same bed with a small child, which he confesses are "due to deeply ingrained taboos and questions" from his past (p. 7).

On the other hand, Brazelton is well aware of all those apparently undamaged Japanese who have grown up co-sleeping with their parents. These days, he also finds himself faced with increasing numbers of American clients—for example, divorced or unwed parents—who feel a "need" to sleep in the same bed with their child. He concludes his remarks by asking, "Should we reevaluate our stance toward children's sleep?" Brazelton's remarks appear in *Ab Initio: An International Newsletter for Professionals Working with Infants and Their Families*. In such an international context, his roomy, inclusive reference to "our stance" is fascinating. It suggests one of the following: (1) that Dr. Brazelton did not ponder fully what it would mean to address such a question to a truly international audience, whose stance on this topic could not be taken for granted, (2) that the actual readership of the "international newsletter" is restricted to professionals from Europe and the United States, or (3) that one measure of being acknowledged as an international "professional" in the infancy field is the adoption of an Anglo-American stance on questions about parent-child co-sleeping.

In any case, before adopting any stance toward co-sleeping arrangements, we might find it helpful to look into the semantics (the form) and pragmatics (the function and distribution) of sleeping arrangements on a worldwide scale. For "our stance," if it refers to the stance of the Anglo-American world, is rather unusual in the international context of family-life practices.

Co-Sleeping Here and There: The American Middle Class and Beyond

Although there have been few systematic studies of co-sleeping between children and their parents in the United States, there does exist a characteristic white middle-class practice concerning who sleeps by whom in the family. Litt (1981), in a pediatric study of 119 children (age six and under) from middle-class, two-parent white families in Cleveland, Ohio, found that only 3 percent of the children regularly slept in their parents' bedroom during the first year of life, and only 1 percent did so after their first birthday. Similar results from an urban sample in California can be found in Rosenfeld and others (1982) and Weisner, Bausano, and Kornfein (1983). Among members of the white middle class, routinized parent-child co-sleeping appears to be exceedingly rare. (Studies of occasional or intermittent parent-child co-sleeping in the white middle class report somewhat higher percentages: Lozoff, Wolf, and Davis, 1984; Mandansky and Edelbrock, 1990.)

Routine parent-child co-sleeping appears to be more common in other U.S. groups. Litt (1981) reports that in Cleveland 55 percent of African-American children less than one year of age co-sleep with a parent every night and all night and that 25 percent of African-American children one to five years of age do so (also see Lozoff, Wolf, and Davis, 1984; Mandansky and Edelbrock, 1990). Abbott (1992), working in a white, predominantly blue-collar community in Appalachian Kentucky, found that 71 percent of children between two months and two years of age and 47 percent of children between two years and four years of age co-slept with a parent. (Abbott does not explicitly state her definition of co-sleeping, although it appears to entail sleeping in a parent's bed or bedroom every night and all night.) Demonstrating that crowding and resource limitations are insufficient explanations of these co-sleeping arrangements, Abbott argues that many blue-collar Appalachian families prefer for parents and their younger children to co-sleep. That preference is articulated in terms of the moral view that the capacity to nurse and nurture are God-given blessings. Co-sleeping is justified as a palpable satisfaction and as an experience of profound "closeness" that enhances the long-term social bonds between parents and their offspring.

The limited research evidence suggests, then, that the sleeping practices of the white middle class have not been uniformly adopted by all groups in the United States. Nevertheless, it also seems reasonable to conclude what most members of the white middle class already know: there exists in white middle-class communities a family-life practice in which, after darkness falls, the bedroom of adults is a private space guarded with taboos against children of all ages and is presumed to be "off limits" (except in the case of occasional medical problems and other emergencies). Children are expected to make it through the night alone.

Of course, anthropologists (see Burton and Whiting, 1961; Caudill and Plath, 1966; LeVine, 1990; Lozoff and Brittenham, 1979; McKenna and others, 1993; Whiting 1964, 1981) have long known that the ritualized isolation and solitude imposed on young children every night in the middle-class Anglo-American culture region are not practiced in most other regions of the world. In Whiting's 1964 survey of "customary" sleeping arrangements in 134 societies, infants and mothers were found to co-sleep most of the time. Commenting on the ethnographic record, Whiting (1981, p. 161) notes that "since in many cultures sleeping arrangements are a private affair, specific ethnographic reports are often lacking and judgments are often made inferentially. . . ." Nevertheless, of the scores of (mostly non-Western, mostly nonindustrial) communities around the world studied by anthropologists on which information is available (Barry and Paxon, 1971), there is not a single community in which infants customarily sleep alone.

Indeed, the historically evolved behavioral script calling for nighttime separation of children from parents that is reenacted on a nightly basis in middle-class American families is often perceived by adults in Africa, Asia, and Central America as a form of "child neglect" (see, for example, Morelli, Rogoff, Oppenheimer, and Goldsmith, 1992). Brazelton himself remarks that the Japanese think of Americans as "merciless" for forcing children to be off on their own and isolated in a dark room throughout the night. Adults in Orissa, India, express similar moral concerns about the practice, which they view as indicative of parental irresponsibility.

Advice Columns and the Moral Perceptions of the Anglo-American Middle Class. Of course, most middle-class Anglo-Americans do not view their own sleeping practices as abusive and immoral. Quite the contrary, they are convinced that their arrangements are sound, are healthy, and promote the moral good. They are disturbed by the practice of parents and children bedding down together at night and nervous about its consequences. They are prone to the view that parent-child co-sleeping is pathological and perhaps even criminal or sinful. Here are two examples of the kinds of queries and responses about parent-child co-sleeping that show up in "expert" advice columns in mainstream middle-class American newspapers such as the *Chicago Tribune.*

> Dear Ann Landers: I have three children, ages 2, 3 and 5. Here's my problem: All three end up in my bedroom during the night. Usually I know they are there but I sleep right through it. . . . I'm newly divorced and there is no man in my bed, so the kids aren't disturbing anyone. . . . My mother tells me I must make the kids sleep in their own rooms. She says sometimes children who want to sleep with their parents need to be taken to a psychologist because their behavior indicates deeper problems. What do you say? Is it that big a deal when they are so young?

Dear Wondering: Usually, I tell parents to keep the kids out of their bed at night, but in your case I suspect the divorce has made them insecure. Talk to your pediatrician about the way to wean these kids away from this habit. You really do need professional guidance. . . . Good luck, dear. You have your hands full. [Jan. 14, 1992]

Dear Abby: I recently spent my first weekend at the home of my fiancé's parents. "Harold" warned me not to be shocked that his 14-year-old younger brother, "Nicky," sleeps in the same bed with their 50-year-old-mother. Needless to say I was appalled. I have always known that Harold's parents have had a troubled marriage and haven't shared a bedroom since 1980. Harold mentioned about a month ago that his younger brother hates sleeping with his mother, but that she threatens to spank him if he sleeps in his own bedroom. Harold has tried talking to his mother about this but she is very irrational and suffers bouts of depression. . . . Someone has to consider the interests of Nicky. I am honestly afraid that this sleeping arrangement could psychologically harm him. Would you please guide me on this issue?

Dear Really Worried: You are to be commended for caring enough to take a stand, because no immediate family member has been willing to become this boy's advocate. Clearly, Nicky is being emotionally blackmailed, and his mother's behavior is inappropriate. You should report her to Children's Services. The number in Texas to call is . . .[Apr. 21, 1992]

After reading about such incidents, a typical middle-class Anglo-American reader is likely to feel full of anxious concerns about issues of sexuality, excessive dependency, and the exploitation of children. Many middle-class Anglo-Americans will be prepared to accept without much reflection the presupposition that the quality of a marriage can be gauged by whether or not a wife and husband sleep together, which is implicit in Really Worried's remarks. Many readers will be offended by the perceived infringements on Nicky's autonomy. They will stigmatize the mother and harbor doubts about her mental health and/or sexual morality. That is a normative and a culturally acceptable response for middle-class Anglo-American readers.

However, it is not a normative or culturally proper response for readers from Japan. Even Dear Abby might be surprised to learn that Japanese parents feel morally obliged to provide their children with a parental sleeping partner; that husbands and wives are willing to separate from each other in order to do so; that approximately 50 percent of eleven- to fifteen-year-old urban Japanese boys and girls sleep in the same room as their mother or father or both; that Japanese fathers are just as likely to co-sleep with their daughters as with their sons; that only 14 percent of eleven- to fifteen-year-olds sleep alone (they sleep with siblings when not co-sleeping with parents); and that no Japanese observer of such practices worries about psychopathology or phones for help (Caudill and Plath, 1966).

The Japanese Case: Where Co-Sleeping Is Normative. The Japanese case is instructive as a lesson in the way cultural practices and individual psychological functioning are intertwined. The classic and most detailed anthropological study of sleeping arrangements is Caudill and Plath's 1966 research report entitled "Who Sleeps by Whom? Parent-Child Involvement in Urban Japanese Families." In their survey of 323 families from the cities of Kyoto, Tokyo, and Matsumoto, Caudill and Plath found that, over a lifetime, a typical Japanese person during the first sixty years of this century seldom slept alone.

It is important to note that the Japanese sleeping practices documented in 1960–1962 were not driven primarily by lack of available space. Caudill and Plath found that three-person households consisting of two parents and an infant did not disperse for sleep even when space was available. For households with more than three persons, variations in available sleeping space accounted for no more than 22 percent of the variance in utilized sleeping space. They concluded that the "Japanese prefer to sleep in clusters of two or three persons and prefer not to sleep alone."

Caudill and Plath suggested that co-sleeping is a source of satisfaction for Japanese children and adults, that Japanese sleeping arrangements "emphasize the interdependency more than the separateness of individuals," and that co-sleeping diminishes the tensions and separations between genders and generations. They even speculate that, given the way culture and psyche make each other up, the practice of sleeping alone is emotionally threatening to the Japanese sense of self and may be a cause of suicide and other psychopathologies.

Co-Sleeping and the Idea of Cultural Practices: Limitations in the Literature

The anthropological and pediatric literature on sleeping practices is not without limitations. The cross-cultural data tend to portray sleeping arrangements in terms of the nuclear triad of mother (m), father (f), and infant or young child (c), without detailed attention to the gender of the child or to the co-sleeping practices of older children. The literature also tends to represent each cultural community with a single "customary" sleeping arrangement, such as mc/f (mother and child co-sleep, father sleeps separately) or mcf (mother, father, and child all sleep together), as though the concept of culture required the investigator to characterize the traditions of a culture in terms of a single fixed sleeping pattern.

This is not the most satisfactory way to conceptualize a "culture" or to study the form and function of sleeping practices. The documentation of patterns of behavior—especially behaviors that are traditional, invested with a moral force, and passed on from generation to generation—is an important first step in the study of culture. However, the study of culture is not reducible to the study of behavior patterns per se. A culture is a way of life lit up by a series of morally enforceable conceptual schemes that are expressed and instantiated in practice. To provide a cultural account, then, one must establish a correspondence between behavior patterns and the preferences, values, moral goods, and causal beliefs exhibited in those behaviors. The entire exercise presupposes that values, meanings, concepts, idea(l)s, and causal beliefs are *analytically* external to and *theoretically* separable from the behaviors themselves. That is why, in the study of sleeping practices discussed below, we conceptualize each recorded instance of who sleeps by whom as a "choice" from a "logical matrix" of possibilities. The "choice" is constrained by a "moral grammar" (an ordered set of cultural preferences, values, and moral goods) that is expressed and realized through the sleeping patterns.

In the remainder of this chapter, we shall employ the following symbols for the designation of kinship statuses: f = father, m = mother, s = son, d = daughter, c = child, number = age in years, / = separate sleeping locations. Within any common sleeping location, the ordering of symbols indicates the ordering of bodies. For example, d7 s3 s8 indicates three co-sleeping children, with the three-year-old son sleeping between the seven-year-old daughter and the eight-year-old son.

We know from our own experience in Orissa, India, that even when there are well-defined cultural values expressed and realized through the practice of who sleeps by whom, there is no "locked-in" single, fixed sleeping pattern. For example, the nuclear relatives of different families might sleep as follows: f d6 / m d3 s4; or f m d4 d7 d9; or f / m d14 d8 s3 / s16.[1] One can, of course, engage in the kind of oversimplification characteristic of much of the previous research on sleeping arrangements by reducing this type of data to summary information about a prototypical nuclear triad (mother, father, child). However, even at that relatively more general level for describing kinship statuses, one still discovers that there is no single, fixed sleeping pattern that characterizes the Oriya community. In our record of single-night sleeping arrangements in 160 households, mcf, mc/f, and mc/fc patterns occur with about equal frequency (27 percent, 29 percent, 25 percent of cases, respectively), and even some instances of mf/c can be observed (12 percent of cases). (The other two possible patterns, m/c/f and fc/m, are rare.)

Nevertheless, as we shall see below, the many sleeping arrangements that do occur in the Oriya community can be coherently understood within the terms of an ordered series of moral goods that define and constrain the "grammatical" variations in behavior that are exhibited. Just as a grammar of a language constrains but does not determine the particular linguistic expressions uttered on any occasion, the moral goods of a culture constrain but do not determine the sleeping arrangements in any particular household.

In other words, the reality and unity of Oriya sleeping practices do not reside at the level of description where we characterize a particular arrangement of bodies on the ground. The reality and unity of the practices reside at the level of description where we characterize the preferences, values, and moral goods realized and expressed by particular arrangements of bodies on the ground. There is no a priori reason to assume that a single ordered set of preferences, values, or moral goods requires all members of a cultural community to arrange themselves in beds in a single way. Furthermore, even when two communities adopt the same sleeping pattern, there is no a priori reason to assume that their behavior realizes and expresses the same moral goods. We shall return to this point later.

Should Parents and Children Co-Sleep? A Moral Debate Without Empirical or Conceptual Foundations

Perhaps the most fascinating feature of the existing literature on sleeping arrangements is that it is packed with moral assumptions and evaluations. Researchers such as Abbott (1992), Caudill and Plath (1966), Brazelton (1990), Gaddini and Gaddini (1970), and Burton and Whiting (1961) have lots of ideas about the consequences of particular sleeping patterns for moral goods such as autonomy, individuation, privacy, group cohesion, sexual freedom, healthy gender identity, and emotional, intellectual and physical well-being. These moral goods are not always explicated or consistently addressed, but they are always relevant to the formulations and explanations offered in the literature.

For example, Whiting (1964) argues that husbands and wives customarily co-sleep in cold climates for the sake of warmth. His analysis thereby presupposes that sleeping arrangements are designed or selected to promote certain moral goods, such as a reduction of physical harm or pain. He assumes that physical comfort (avoiding the cold) is a good reason for co-sleeping with a spouse and might even explain why people in cold climates stay in bed together through the night.

A few researchers go a step further and take an interest in the moral reasons people actually adduce as the motive for their sleeping arrangements (for example, Morelli, Rogoff, Oppenheimer, and Goldsmith, 1992). It is not unusual for anthropological researchers to contextualize cultural sleeping practices by presenting readers with some verbal justifications offered by a few local informants, although it is the rare study indeed whose central focus is the way members of a community think about the relationship between who sleeps by whom and the moral order. Abbott (1992, p. 34), for example, quotes a local Appalachian writer who morally justifies the practice of mother-child co-sleeping by remarking, "How can you expect to hold on to them in later life if you begin their lives by pushing them away?"

Other authors, such as Brazelton (1990) (and Ann Landers and Dear Abby, of course), express their own moral views about whether this or that pattern of co-sleeping is justified or not. This type of moral discourse seems unavoidable if we are to credit the bearers of a cultural tradition with agency and with the capacity for responsible and rational action, unless we are prepared to defend the antirationalist proposition that "the examined life is not worth living." When Brazelton asks, "Should we re-evaluate our stance toward children's sleep?" he is raising a Socratic question that no responsible and reflective participant in the life of a family can avoid. Although Brazelton's question should not be evaded, we think it is best to put off answering it for a while. There is no point in engaging in a full-blown moral debate about who should sleep by whom until some firm empirical and conceptual foundations for the debate have been put in place.

With regard to the empirical foundations that need to be put in place, both those who condemn and those who justify parent-child co-sleeping arrangements make many assumptions about objective means-ends connections. Yet systematic evidence is almost never presented (and may not exist) on whether co-sleeping in childhood per se in fact deepens long-term familial cohesion, whether sleeping alone since infancy per se in fact promotes independence and autonomy in adulthood, or whether witnessing the primal scene per se in fact is a cause of neuroses in adulthood. (For discrepant opinions of the dangers of viewing the primal scene, see Dahl, 1982, and Rosenfeld and others, 1980.)

It is conceivable that particular sleeping practices per se have no predictable long-term effects on individual psychological functioning and character formation. Sleeping practices may serve mainly as daily ritual enactments of the fundamental values of a group and/or as a measure used by insiders for determining who should be accepted as "normal" and "cooperative" members of that society.

It is conceivable that, even if sleeping arrangements per se have no long-term effect on individual psychological functioning and character formation, sleeping arrangements may have long-term effects that are predictable once the local meaning of the practice has been taken into account. In other words, the effects of a sleeping practice may be largely mediated by the moral meaning conferred on the practice by a group. Perhaps it is being confronted with a culturally deviant behavior in the bedroom (enforced isolation in a Japanese family; enforced co-sleeping in an Anglo-American family) that puts a child at risk.

It is also conceivable that any long-term effects of a particular sleeping arrangement on the emotional life of a particular individual are entirely idiosyncratic and involve a complex interaction between details of the practice and aspects of personal temperament (see Kakar, 1990, for a relevant clinical case from India). Unfortunately, given the state of the research evidence, no one really knows whether any of these conceivable alternatives are true. From an empirical point of view, international moral advisers on sleeping arrangements are simply explicating their local cultural intuitions while skating on thin evidential ice.

From a conceptual point of view, the foundations for addressing the question, Who ought to sleep by whom in the family? are no more secure. Those who condemn and those who justify parent-child co-sleeping arrangements make many strong and limiting assumptions about moral goods. Yet rarely are those moral considerations informed by a systematic examination of the range of moral values that are exhibited in the sleeping practices of different cultures around the world. Rarely is the problem of who should sleep by whom conceptualized as a problem in choosing between alternative, and perhaps conflicting, moral goods. While the research to be reported below will not provide an answer to Brazelton's question about who ought to sleep by whom, it may supply some conceptual and empirical fuel for the moral debate already begun.

Who Sleeps by Whom in Orissa and Hyde Park?

Method and Data. Three types of data are discussed in the sections that follow: (1) the results of a "sleeping arrangement task" in which informants in Orissa, India, and Hyde Park, Illinois, sorted members of a hypothetical seven-person family into sleeping spaces under various hypothetical resource constraints; (2) the results of a "preference conflict task" in which informants in Orissa, India, and Hyde Park, Illinois, evaluated and ranked various culturally deviant arrangements of members of the hypothetical seven-person family in terms of the relative seriousness of the breach; (3) spot reports about who slept by whom on a single night in 160 households in the Hindu temple town of Bhubaneswar in Orissa, India.[2]

Extracting Moral Goods: The Logical Matrix of the Sleeping Arrangement Task. In our view, sleeping arrangements are a joint product of cultural preferences (for example, the particular moral goods promoted by a people) and local resource constraints (for example, the amount of space available). Given our conceptualization of sleeping arrangements as symbolic actions, our main concern is to extract similarities and differences in cultural preferences, values, or goods as they are revealed in practice, while taking account of similarities or differences that are driven primarily by limited space.

Oriya and American informants were presented with a sleeping arrangement task. For this task, a hypothetical family was constructed consisting of seven members: f, m, s15, s11, s8, d14, and d3. Nineteen Oriya adults (eleven women and eight men) and nineteen American adults (nine women and ten men) were asked to arrange members of the family into separate sleeping spaces under different hypothetical resource constraints. You have one room. How would you arrange the seven family members? You have two rooms. And so forth through seven rooms. At each resource level, the informant was free to declare that no sorting was possible or desirable. Informants were also asked to select their most preferred resource level: How many separate sleeping rooms would be ideal for this seven-person family?

An important first step in the cultural analysis of the proposed solutions to the sleeping arrangement task given by Oriya and American informants is the elaboration of a "logical matrix." A logical matrix for the sleeping arrangement task is a characterization of all the logically possible ways to arrange the members of a seven-person family into from one to seven discrete sleeping spaces. In total, there are 877 logically possible ways to do that. Of course, there is only one way to sort seven persons into one room, and only one way to sort seven persons into seven rooms. But there are 63 logically possible ways to sort seven persons into two rooms, 301 ways for 3 rooms, 350 ways for four rooms, 140 ways for five rooms, and 21 ways for 6 rooms. (See Table 2.1 [top half] for an example of the calculation of the logically possible ways to sort seven persons into three rooms.)

It is a crucial fact about the force of cultural constraints on the practice of who sleeps by whom that exceedingly few of the 877 logically possible solutions were selected by any Oriya or American informant. For example, no one ever proposed such four-room solutions as f d14 / m s15 / s8 d3 / s11 or m / f d3 / s15 d14 / s8 s11. No one ever proposed such a two-room solution as d3 / f m s15 d14 s11 s8. Indeed, perhaps 95 percent of the possible solutions in the logical matrix were (and would always be) ruled out as immoral, unacceptable, or otherwise "ungrammatical" by informants in both cultures. We would predict that even with a very large sample of informants, very few solutions (fewer than 15 or so out of 877) would be selected with any frequency by informants in either culture. We would also predict that the small subset of solutions selected by Oriya Indians would not be coincidental with those selected by Americans.

Consider, for example, the Oriya and American solutions to the sleeping arrangement task under the two-room constraint. Sixteen of nineteen Oriya informants offered a solution. Despite the fact that there are 63 logically possible ways to sort the family into two rooms, 75 percent of those Oriya informants selected one of two solutions: f s15 s11 s8 / m d14 d3 or f s15 s11 / m d14 d3 s8. In stark contrast, only seven of nineteen American informants were able to offer a solution at all under the two-room constraint. Almost all of them converged on a sleeping arrangement that no Oriya chose—namely, f m d14 d3 / s15 s11 s8.

Table 2.1. Distribution of Logically Possible Solutions and Actually Selected Solutions to the Sleeping Arrangement Task Under the Three-Room Constraint

Persons per Space	1/1/5	1/2/4	1/3/3	2/2/3
Number of possible solutions (Total = 301)	21	105	70	105
Frequency of Selection				
Oriyas	0	0	2	17
Americans	0	0	1	17

	Oriyas	Americans
Most Favored 2/2/3 Splits		
f m / d14 d3 / s15 s11 s8	8	15
f m d3 / d14 s8 / s15 s11	4	0
f s8 / s15 s11 / m d14 d3	4	0
f m / s15 s11 / d14 d3 s8	1	1
s11 s8 / s15 d14 / f m d3	0	1

Preferences, Values, and Moral Goods of Two Cultures. There is a small set of cultural preferences that can help us explain the many unselected possibilities from the logical matrix. At least one of those relevant moral preferences will be familiar to all students of family dynamics. That preference can be summarized under the principle of "incest avoidance": within the family, sexualized unmarried males and females must not have sex with each other and should avoid all situations, such as co-sleeping, where there may be sexual temptations or even suspicions about sexual contact. It seems likely that incest avoidance is a universal moral preference, although allowances must be made for cultural variations in the scope of incest avoidance beyond the nuclear family and in the age of the people who must be separated.

Some of the other relevant moral preferences are more culture-specific. One such preference can be summarized under the principle of "female chastity anxiety": in a culture such as India, where it is important in the context of marriage arrangements for unmarried sexualized women to be chaste, young unmarried girls are constantly chaperoned. Thus they should not sleep alone at night. Another preference can be summarized under the principle of "respect for hierarchy": among sexually mature males, social superiority is expressed through deference and distance, which is incompatible with the intimacy, familiarity, and exposure of co-sleeping. Still another moral preference falls under the principle of "protection of the vulnerable": highly valued members of the family, such as children who are needy and fragile and should not be left alone at night.

There is also a preference that can be summarized under the ideal of "autonomy": highly valued members of the family, such as children, are needy and fragile and should be encouraged to be alone at night so that they can learn to be self-reliant and independent and to care for themselves. A final moral preference falls under the principle of "the sacred couple": when it comes to co-habiting adults, emotional intimacy, interpersonal commitment, and sexual privacy require that they sleep together and alone.

Each of these principles is a constraint on who sleeps by whom at night, although their interpretation and application leave room for local cultural discretion. For example, under Oriya interpretations, the incest avoidance principle requires separate sleeping space for at least these pairs: (f / d14), (m / s15), (s15 / d14). Under American interpretations, given the influence of certain ethnopsychological doctrines about the sexualized character of interactions between young children and adults, the moral preference for incest avoidance might require separate sleeping space for other pairs too: (m / s11), (m/ s8), (s11 / d14), (s8 / d14), and (f / d3).

For Oriyas, there are four moral preferences implicit in their choices on the sleeping arrangement task: incest avoidance, protection of the vulnerable, female chastity anxiety, and respect for hierarchy. Thus, for example, a logically possible sleeping arrangement such as that proposed by an American informant—m f / s15 / d14 / d3 / s11 s8—is ruled out by Oriya informants because it is inconsistent with two important local moral preferences: female chastity anxiety (d14 cannot sleep alone) and protection of the vulnerable (d3 cannot sleep alone).

For middle-class Anglo-Americans, in contrast, there are three moral preferences, values, or goods implicit in their choices on the sleeping arrangement task: incest avoidance, the sacred couple, and autonomy. Thus, for example, a logically possible sleeping arrangement such as the one proposed by an Oriya informant—f / m s8 / d14 d3 / s15 s11—is ruled out by American informants because it is inconsistent with two important local moral preferences: the sacred couple (m and f should have exclusive co-sleeping space) and autonomy (each child should sleep alone).

Ordering of Moral Goods on the Preference Conflict Task. We are doubtful that the choices favoring a partitioning of sleeping locations in Oriya and American households are ever fully contravened by resource constraints. Even in a relatively confined space, members of a family can divide themselves into separate sleeping areas (using, for example, mats, beds, sections of a floor). Nevertheless, from an analytic point of view, it is useful to imagine occasions when sleeping space is limited and members of a culture must make choices among their moral preferences. The preferences for each culture can be arranged in a precedence order, as we have done below.

This ordering was determined by presenting informants with the preference conflict task. In this task, four Oriya adults and sixteen American adults were asked to rank a set of sleeping patterns selected to exemplify breaches of the various moral preferences or goods in each culture. All the offensive arrangements had reference to the same seven-person family used in the sleeping arrangement task. The preference conflict task was administered only after the groups' moral preferences and goods had been extracted by means of the sleeping arrangement task. Table 2.2 lists the various offensive arrangements presented to informants in Orissa and Hyde Park. They are ordered from "most offensive" to "least offensive," based on the aggregate or average results from the preference conflict task in the two cultures.

It appears that Oriya moral preferences can be listed in order of importance as follows: incest avoidance, protection of the vulnerable, female chastity anxiety, respect for hierarchy. For example, as shown in Table 2.2, a breach such as f d14 / m d3 / s11 s8 / s15 (a strong violation of incest avoidance) is judged by Oriyas to be more severe than a breach such as d14 / f / m d3 / s15 s11 s8 (a strong violation of female chastity anxiety), which in turn is judged to be more severe than a breach such as f s15 / m d14 d3 / s11 s8 (a strong violation of respect for hierarchy).

Given the content of middle-class American moral preferences and the structure of the seven-person family, it was not easy to select a neatly discriminating set of breaches for the preference conflict task. We recognize that the particular set of offending arrangements presented to American informants (and shown in Table 2.2) is not ideal for determining the full ordering of American moral preferences. Nevertheless, it is our hypothesis that middle-class American moral preferences can be listed in order of importance as follows:

**Table 2.2. Culturally Offensive Sleeping Arrangements
Ranked by Informants in Order of Severity of Breach**

Orissa, India

f dl4 / m d3 / sll s8 / s15
d3 / f / m dl4 / s15 sll s8
s8 d3 / f / m dl4 / s15 sll
dl4 / f / m d3 / s15 sll s8
m / f / dl4 d3 / s15 sll s8
dl4 sll / f / m d3 / s15 s8
f s15 / m dl4 d3 / sll s8
f sll / m d3 / s15 / dl4 s8
f s15 / m d3 / dl4 s8 / sll

Hyde Park, United States

f dl4 / m s15 / sll / s8 / d3
f m / s15 dl4 / sll / s8 / d3
f s15 / m dl4 / sll / s8 / d3
f / m / dl4 d3 / s15 s8 / sll

Note: All these arrangements are offensive or "ungrammatical" to some degree in the relevant culture. Rankings move from most morally offensive at the top to least morally offensive at the bottom.

incest avoidance, the sacred couple, autonomy. One source of support for part of this hypothesis can be seen in Table 2.2, where a breach such as f m / s15 dl4 / sll / s8 / d3 (a violation of incest avoidance) is judged by Americans to be more severe than a breach such as f / m / dl4 d3 / s15 s8 / sll (a violation of both the sacred couple principle and the principle of autonomy). A second source of support comes from the sleeping arrangement task, where American informants often sacrificed the principle of autonomy while honoring the exclusive sleeping rights of the conjugal couple as required by the sacred couple principle. More work needs to be done to establish the precedence ordering of American values, however.

The Cultural Component of Sleeping Practices: There Is More to Who Sleeps by Whom Than Resource Constraints. Notice that there are both similarities and differences in the preferences implicit in the judgments of informants from Orissa, India, and Hyde Park, Illinois. The single most important moral preference in both cultures is the same: incest avoidance. All the other moral preferences differentiate the two cultures. For example, the second most important preference for middle-class Americans—what we have dubbed the sacred couple—plays no part in the choices made in the Oriya culture. This American sacred couple principle alone places such a great constraint on possible solutions to the sleeping arrangement task that it rules out 92 percent of the 877 possible cells in the logical matrix; indeed, at certain resource levels, Americans can conceive of fewer solutions than the Oriyas. Thus many Oriyas are willing to accept a two-room solution that divides males (f s15 sll s8) from females (m dl4 d3) and honors the incest avoidance principle. But this arrangement violates the sacred couple principle for Americans, and thus most Americans find it unacceptable.

The results of our study make it apparent why in constructing an analysis of a practice it is imperative to distinguish between cultural preferences and resource constraints. Under particular resource constraints, the sleeping practices of two communities may look more similar than an analysis of cultural preferences would reveal. Thus, for example, Oriya Hindus and Hyde Park Americans tend to converge in their solutions to the sleeping arrangement task under the three-room constraint, despite the fact that their choices are regulated by somewhat different moral preferences. Under the three-room resource constraint, both Americans and Oriyas tend to favor f m / d14 d3 / s15 s11 s8. This is shown in Table 2.1 (bottom half). As indicated in Table 2.1, this arrangement is only one of 301 logically possible ways to divide seven persons into three rooms, and it is only one of 105 logically possible ways to divide the persons into a two-two-three person-per-room arrangement. Yet that one arrangement is preferred by a vast majority of American informants as well as by a plurality of the Oriya informants.

This particular sleeping arrangement is consistent with the two most important middle-class American moral preferences (incest avoidance and the sacred couple). Under a three-room constraint, most American informants seem willing to compromise on the autonomy of the children. The arrangement is also consistent with the three most important Oriya moral goods (incest avoidance, protection of the vulnerable, and female chastity anxiety). (While there is no sacred couple principle in force in Orissa, the local culture does not prohibit exclusive parental co-sleeping, as long as culturally relevant principles are honored.) Under the three-room constraint, Oriyas seem willing to compromise on respect for hierarchy, although it might be argued that that principle applies only to the relationship of f and s15, in which case the willingness to accept co-sleeping for s15, s11, and s8 may not be a compromise after all.

Under the three-room resource constraint, Oriyas do generate some solutions that middle-class Americans reject, such as f s8 / s15 s11 / m d14 d3 (see Table 2.1). Nevertheless, if one were to observe only the behavior of the two cultures at that one resource level, one might be misled into thinking that the two cultures were more or less the same. Only when one looks at behavior across a variety of resource constraints are differences in cultural preferences, values, and moral goods revealed. The implication of this finding is important enough to warrant restating: in the face of any particular resource constraint, two different moral preference systems may give rise to similar "on the ground" sleeping arrangements; therefore, mere "on the ground" observation is insufficient as a method for determining cultural differences.

Actual Sleeping Arrangements in the Temple Town: 160 Spot Reports. How relevant is our account of Oriya preferences to "on the ground" sleeping arrangements in the temple town? In order to answer this question, we tested the Oriya and American packages of moral preferences on our corpus of spot reports.

Interviews were conducted with 160 children (ages eight to twelve) and adults, who were asked to describe the sleeping locations of members of their family on the previous night. We relied on interviews rather than observations, as it is not feasible to enter the interior spaces of a Hindu family compound to observe who sleeps by whom. We will treat these spot reports as though they were a behavioral case record, although ultimately we have no way to assess the degree of memory distortion, idealization, or error in this verbal record.

Twelve cases of nighttime sleeping arrangement, randomly selected from the data set, are listed in Table 2.3. As should be obvious from that table, the family co-sleeping networks in the temple town rarely fit the standard middle-class Anglo-American pattern.

Several decisions had to be made about precisely how to apply the various moral preference principles to the 160 cases at hand. These decisions were resolved in the following ways: (1) the Oriya female chastity principle is applied only to unmarried sexualized females, and the principle is not violated whenever an unmarried sexualized female shares a room with another family member, no matter who that is; (2) the Oriya respect for hierarchy principle does not apply between sons but only between father and son; (3) the incest avoidance principle does not apply to co-sleeping of grandparents and grand-children; (4) the principles of incest avoidance, female chastity anxiety, and respect for hierarchy are violated only if the child of relevance is thirteen years of age or older. Finally, in order to simplify our analysis, we treated all indige-nously recognized separations of sleeping space (different mats on two sides of a courtyard, different beds on two sides of a partition, different rooms) as equivalent separations.

In 87 percent of the Oriya households, sleeping arrangements were con-sistent with all four Oriya preferences. The most important principle, incest

Table 2.3. Spot Reports of Previous Night's Sleeping Arrangement in Twelve Oriya Households

Space	Sleeping Arrangement	Persons per Space
1	f d5 d7 m	4
2	f / s9 d6 d1 m	1/4
2	f / d12 s10 s8 d4 m s15	1/6
2	f / s5 m s4 d7 d10 d13 d16	1/7
2	f s4 s7 / m d10 fm	3/3
2	f s9 m s6 / s18	4/1
3	f / m d6 s10 / s16	1/3/1
3	f s6 / m s4 / fm	2/2/1
3	f m / s12 d7 d15/ ff	2/3/1
3	f s10 s6 / s20 / m (menstruating)	3/1/1
4	f / ff / m d10 d12 d14 / s12 s15 s16	1/1/4/3
4	f m d6 / s9 s14 / s16 s19 / fm	3/2/2/1

Note: The twelve households were randomly chosen from 160 spot reports. f = father, m = mother, s = son, d = daughter, fm = father's mother, ff = father's father, number following s or d = age of child, / = separation of sleeping space. Within a common sleeping space, the order of symbols is the order of sleeping positions.

avoidance, was violated in 8 of 160 households. An example of a violation of the incest avoidance principle can be found in Table 2.3 (line 3), where the mother and her fifteen-year-old son co-sleep, although in the presence of four other children (f / d12 s10 s8 d4 m s15). Based on the results of our sleeping arrangement task, members of the local Oriya community might well look askance at that particular arrangement, although within the terms of Oriya ethnopsychology it may not be easy to set precise age boundaries on the upper limits for nonexclusive parent-child co-sleeping. The second most important principle, protection of the vulnerable, was never violated. The third most important principle, female chastity anxiety, was violated in two households. The principle of respect for hierarchy was violated in twelve households.

It is a useful exercise to apply the package of American moral preferences to the actual Oriya sleeping arrangements. The American sacred couple principle was violated in 78 percent of Oriya households. Indeed, actual sleeping arrangements in the temple town were consistent with all three American preferences in only 11 percent of the cases.

Conclusion: The Meaning of Practice

We began this chapter by examining two questions posed by the pediatrician T. Berry Brazelton: Should we reevaluate our stance toward children's sleep, and who ought to sleep by whom in the family? It has not been our aim to answer these questions. Instead, we have tried to point to some of the conceptual and empirical work that needs to be done before these questions can be seriously addressed. Who sleeps by whom is not merely a personal or private activity. It is a social practice, like burying the dead or eating meals with your family or honoring the practice of a monogamous marriage, which (for those engaged in the practice) is invested with moral and social meaning and with implications for a person's standing in a community. Those meanings and implications must be taken into account if the issue of who sleeps by whom is to be treated not so much as a mindless habit or tradition-laden routine but as a deliberate act of rational choice motivated by an analysis of probable psychological and social costs and benefits.

In this chapter, we have presented a method (the application of a logical matrix) for identifying some of the moral and social meanings implicit in the practice of who sleeps by whom. We have examined similarities and differences in the preferred moral goods (for example, incest avoidance, the sacred couple, protection of the vulnerable) of two culture regions (rural Hindu India and urban middle-class white America). Much work still remains to be done examining the effects, if any, of particular sleeping practices on the development of competence in various domains of psychological functioning (emotional, moral, interpersonal, cognitive) (see LeVine, 1990). Likewise, much work still remains to be done examining the developmental advantages, if any, of growing up in a family that engages in culturally consensual sleeping practices (co-sleeping, if you are an Oriya child; sleeping alone if you are a middle-class Anglo-American child). Nevertheless, on the basis of what we already know about the cultural meanings implicit in family-life practices, no informed discussion of parent-child co-sleeping can proceed unless those involved in the discussion first recognize that behavior per se is not what the action is about. The family order is part of the social order, which is part of the moral order—which is why (in Japan, in South Asia, even in the Anglo-American culture region) a cultural analysis of local preferences, values, and moral goods is a necessary first step in making sense of who sleeps by whom.

Notes

1. Oriya family households are either joint or nucleated. When they are joint, two or more adult brothers co-reside (with their parents, if the parents are still alive), and the brothers' wives and children all live together in a single patrilocal family home or compound. In our data, which were based on reports from children and adults, the co-sleeping network for a child almost never included that child's aunts, uncles, cousins, or father's father, although children did sometimes co-sleep with their father's mother. The father's father rarely co-slept with a child and most often slept alone, separated from his wife.
2. The first type of data was collected in 1983 (from Oriya informants) and in 1991 (from American informants). The second type of data was collected in 1991 from both Oriya and American informants. The third type of data was collected in Orissa, India, in 1983. (For a discussion of the moral basis of family and social-life practices in Bhubaneswar, see Mahapatra, 1981; Shweder, 1991; Shweder, Mahapatra, and Miller, 1987; Shweder, Much, Mahapatra, and Park, in press.)

References

Abbott, S. "Holding On and Pushing Away: Comparative Perspectives on an Eastern Kentucky Child-Rearing Practice." *Ethos*, 1992, *1*, 33–65.

Barry, H., and Paxon, L. M. "Infancy and Early Childhood: Cross-Cultural Codes 2." *Ethnology*, 1971, *10*, 466–508.

Brazelton, T. B. "Parent-Infant Cosleeping Revisited." *Ab Initio: An International Newsletter for Professionals Working with Infants and Their Families*, 1990, *1*, 1, 7.

Burton, R. V., and Whiting, J.W.M. "The Absent Father and Cross-Sex Identity." *Merrill-Palmer Quarterly*, 1961, *7*, 85–95.

Caudill, W., and Plath, D. W. "Who Sleeps by Whom? Parent-Child Involvement in Urban Japanese Families." *Psychiatry*, 1966, *29*, 344–366.

Dahl, G. "Notes on Critical Examinations of the Primal Scene Concept." *Journal of the American Psychoanalytic Association*, 1982, *30*, 657–677.

Gaddini, R., and Gaddini, E. "Transitional Objects and the Process of Individualization: A Study in Three Different Groups." *American Academy of Clinical Psychiatry*, 1970, *9*, 347–365.

Kakar, S. "Stories from Indian Psychoanalysis: Text and Context." In J. W. Stigler, R. A. Shweder, and G. Herdt (eds.), *Cultural Psychology: Essays on Comparative Human Development*. New York: Cambridge University Press, 1990.

LeVine, R. A. "Infant Environments in Psychoanalysis: A Cross-Cultural View." In J. W. Stigler, R. A. Shweder, and G. Herdt (eds.), *Cultural Psychology: Essays on Comparative Human Development*. New York: Cambridge University Press, 1990.

Litt, C. J. "Children's Attachment to Transitional Objects: A Study of Two Pediatric Populations." *American Journal of Orthopsychiatry*, 1981, *51*, 131–139.

Lozoff, B., and Brittenham, G. "Infant Care: Cache or Carry." *Behavioral Pediatrics*, 1979, *95*, 478–483.

Lozoff, B., Wolf, A. W., and Davis, N. S. "Cosleeping in Urban Families with Young Children in the United States." *Pediatrics,* 1984, *74,* 171–182.

McKenna, J. J., and others. "Infant-Parent Co-Sleeping in an Evolutionary Perspective: Implications for Understanding Infant Sleep Development and the Sudden Infant Death Syndrome." *Sleep,* 1993, *16,* 263–282.

Mahapatra, M. *Traditional Structure and Change in an Orissan Temple.* Calcutta: Punthi Pustak, 1981.

Mandansky, D., and Edelbrock, C. "Cosleeping in a Community Sample of 2- and 3-Year-Old Children." *Pediatrics,* 1990, *86,* 197–203.

Morelli, G. A., Rogoff, B., Oppenheimer, D., and Goldsmith, D. "Cultural Variations in Infants' Sleeping Arrangements: Question of Independence." *Developmental Psychology,* 1992, *28,* 604–613.

Rosenfeld, and others. "The Primal Scene: A Study of Prevalence." *American Journal of Psychiatry,* 1980, *137,* 1426–1428.

Rosenfeld, and others. "Sleeping Patterns in Upper Middle-Class Families When the Child Awakens Ill or Frightened." *Archives of General Psychiatry,* 1982, *39,* 943–947.

Shweder, R. A. *Thinking Through Cultures: Expeditions in Cultural Psychology.* Cambridge, Mass.: Harvard University Press, 1991.

Shweder, R. A., Mahapatra, M., and Miller, J. G. "Culture and Moral Development." In J. Kagan and S. Lamb (eds.), *The Emergence of Morality in Young Children.* Chicago: University of Chicago Press, 1987.

Shweder, R. A., Much, N. C., Mahapatra, M., and Park, L. "The 'Big Three' of Morality (Autonomy, Community, Divinity), and the 'Big Three' Explanations of Suffering." In A. Brandt and P. Rozin (eds.), *Morality and Health.* Stanford, Calif: Stanford University Press, in press.

Weisner, T. S., Bausano, M., and Kornfein, M. "Putting Family Ideals into Practice." *Ethos,* 1983, *11,* 278–304.

Whiting, J.W.M. "Effects of Climate on Certain Cultural Practices." In W. H. Goodenough (ed.), *Explorations in Cultural Anthropology.* New York: McGraw-Hill, 1964.

Whiting, J.W.M. "Environmental Constraints on Infant Care Practices." In R. H. Munroe, R. L. Munroe, and B. B. Whiting (eds.), *Handbook of Cross-Cultural Human Development.* New York: Garland, 1981.

RICHARD A. SHWEDER *is professor of human development and chair, Committee on Human Development, University of Chicago.*

LENE ARNETT JENSEN *is a doctoral candidate, Committee on Human Development, University of Chicago.*

WILLIAM M. GOLDSTEIN *is associate professor, Department of Psychology and Committee on Human Development, University of Chicago.*

Editors' Preface to "Development Through Participation in Sociocultural Activity"

The following chapter focuses primarily on the proposition that development is a process of transformation through participation in cultural practices. Beginning with the assumption that change is inherent in cultural practices, the authors argue that when a practice, rather than the individual, is taken as the unit of analysis, a broader, more diversified, and yet more integrated understanding of development becomes possible—one that necessarily encompasses multiple analytic perspectives. The chapter builds upon approaches to development that emphasize shifts over time in a novice's participation in a task—shifts captured in the metaphor of learning as apprenticeship (Lave, 1988; Rogoff, 1990), in the description of individual change as a move from peripheral to full participation (Lave and Wenger, 1991), and in the analysis of learning as based upon a process of "guided participation" (Rogoff, 1990; Rogoff, Mistry, Göncü, and Mosier, 1993) or upon a process of "scaffolding" by which the expert provides and withdraws support in a manner linked to the learner's changing competence (for example, Wertsch, McNamee, McLane, and Budwig, 1980; Wood, Bruner, and Ross, 1976). In these approaches, change occurs both in the learner and in the interpersonal relationship between the novice/learner and the mentor/expert. (A review chapter from the Laboratory of Comparative Human Cognition, 1983, and a broad-ranging book—Forman, Minick, and Stone, 1993—bring out the wide variety of studies that reflect these perspectives.)

To that approach, Rogoff, Baker-Sennett, Lacasa, and Goldsmith now add a new component. What needs to be considered, they propose, are three forms of change: changes in the child's participation (personal plane), changes in the relationship between participants (interpersonal plane), and historical changes in technologies and institutions (community plane). Moreover, changes at any one of these levels cannot be explained without reference to the other levels.

How are researchers to meet the challenge of considering changes at all three levels? Rogoff and her colleagues take on that challenge in their chapter, basing their discussion on a study of Girl Scout cookie sales. By foregrounding first the community level of analysis—how the history of cookies sales has changed over the years—and then the individual level of analysis—how the participation of child newcomers to the practice changes—they show that community and individual development are co-constituted through sociocultural activity.

This notion of co-constitution threads through much of the literature on cultural practices, often with little explication of exactly what is meant by the term. Rogoff and her colleagues illustrate a way of specifying this process, showing how historical changes create the conditions for individual development and how individual development creates the conditions for historical development. For example, the introduction of color-coded order forms (a change in technology at the community level) redefined how succeeding generations of girls have kept track of cookie sales. (This is not to say that every child will use the form in identical ways, but that a troop's adoption of this tool sets the parameters for the cognitive tasks that girls will routinely encounter.) At the same time, innovations in the collective practice of Girl Scout cookies sales have been brought about by individuals. Juliette Low founded the Scout movement in the United States in 1912. Bella Spewack (and others) invented the Girl Scout cookie in the 1920s. Older Scouts in the 1990s are beginning to appropriate electronic mail as a tool for reaching more customers.

Devising new forms of participation is only one way in which individuals constitute community practice. Rogoff and her colleagues also underscore a fundamental fact of social life that is rarely acknowledged in theories of human development—namely, that the maintenance of culture is an ongoing accomplishment. This is one of the major insights of practice theory. Without the continuing participation of individual children (as well as parents, troop leaders, and customers), the tradition of selling Girl Scout cookies would die out. In this sense, the continued vitality of this practice over many decades, despite major social changes (for example, the influx of mothers into the labor force), is an achievement that cannot be taken for granted.

Indeed, in many communities in the United States and around the world, cultural practices are disappearing, sometimes with extraordinary rapidity (see, for example, Heath, 1990; Herdt, 1987). Don Kulick's (1992) work on language shift in Papua, New Guinea, is a case in point. Kulick offers an analysis of change in the nature of a practice (the loss of the local language of Taiap from one generation to the next) combined with attention to the way this change is linked to interpersonal relationships: the older children are the major teachers of the younger ones, and the older children are moving toward using the national pidgin, influenced both by school practices and by their parents' use of the local language for "homely" scenes (for example, expressions of anger toward neighbors) and pidgin for topics of "significance." This change has occurred even though adults regard Taiap as an important marker of identity, distinguishing them from the neighboring tribes with their languages. Kulick's study thus demonstrates that even practices that have strong historical roots in a culture and embody deeply held values are vulnerable to disruption and loss.

The message for developmentalists is that broadening our perspective to encompass community trajectories of change challenges basic assumptions about the developmental process. For example, development does not necessarily involve a linear progression. Children are not simply cultural novices en route to adult-level mastery of cultural knowledge. They are producers of culture in their own right.

This view of children goes far beyond the usual characterization of children as "active." In the discourse of modern developmental psychology, children are often cast as active constructors of knowledge, not passive recipients of cultural givens. It is also widely recognized that interactional influences flow both ways, from parent to child and from child to parent. Although a practice perspective embraces both of these assumptions, it also acknowledges that children produce and maintain culture by participating in everyday practices. This point has been demonstrated in recent studies of peer culture (for example, Eder and Sanford, 1986; Goodwin, 1990). It is also at the heart of Corsaro's (1992) ethnographic studies in nursery schools in the United States and Italy, which demonstrate that children do not directly appropriate adult culture but rather creatively reinterpret and transform adult practices to produce their own unique peer cultures. He argues that developmental theorists' preoccupation with the individual process of internalization of adult culture obscures the collective process by which children become a part of culture through their negotiations with adults and their creative production with other children of a series of age-graded peer cultures. The implication is that development involves successive reorganizations of children's social worlds.

Rogoff, Baker-Sennett, Lacasa, and Goldsmith take a very similar view of development as transformation. In fact, one of the major conceptual tasks of their chapter is to distinguish transformation from acquisition. It is important to emphasize that these authors' conception of transformation is quite different from classic notions of developmental stages. What gets transformed is not abstract knowledge structures but both participation itself and the relationships among participants. Like Lave and Wenger (1991), these authors argue that newcomers to a practice move from peripheral participation to full participation, from less responsible to more responsible roles. These transformations are paralleled by changes in the participant as a *person*—an acting, knowing, and valuing being with a sense of place and identity in the community. When one begins with the person-participating-in-a-practice, rather than the individual isolated from context, a more holistic and unified understanding of the person becomes possible.

References

Corsaro, W. A. "Interpretive Reproduction in Children's Peer Cultures." *Social Psychology Quarterly*, 1992, 55 (2), 160–177.

Eder, D., and Sanford, S. "The Development and Maintenance of Interactional Norms Among Early Adolescents." In P. A. Adler and P. Adler (eds.), *Sociological Studies of Child Development*. Vol. 1. Greenwich, Conn. Jai Press, 1986.

Forman, E. A., Minick, N., and Stone, C. A. (eds.). *Contexts for Learning: Socio-Cultural Dynamics in Children's Development*. New York: Oxford University Press, 1993.

Goodwin, M. H. *He-Said-She-Said: Talk as Social Organization Among Black Children*. Bloomington: Indiana University Press, 1990.

Heath, S. B. "The Children of Trackton's Children: Spoken and Written Language in Social Change." In J. W. Stigler, R. A. Shweder, and G. Herdt (eds.), *Cultural Psychology: Essays on Comparative Human Development*. New York: Cambridge University Press, 1990.

Herdt, G. H. *The Sambia: Ritual and Gender in New Guinea*. Troy, Mo.: Holt, Rinehart & Winston, 1987.

Kulick, D. *Language Shift and Cultural Reproduction: Socialization, Self, and Syncretism in a Papua New Guinean Village*. New York: Cambridge University Press, 1992.

Laboratory of Comparative Human Cognition. "Culture and Cognitive Development." In W. Kessen (ed.), *Mussen's Handbook of Child Psychology*. Vol. 1. (4th ed.) New York: Wiley, 1983.

Lave, J. *Cognition in Practice: Mind, Mathematics, and Culture in Everyday Life*. New York: Cambridge University Press, 1988.

Lave, J., and Wenger, E. *Situated Learning: Legitimate Peripheral Participation*. New York: Cambridge University Press, 1991.

Rogoff, B. *Apprenticeship in Thinking: Cognitive Development in Social Context*. New York: Oxford University Press, 1990.

Rogoff, B., Mistry, J. J., Göncü, A., and Mosier, C. *Guided Participation in Cultural Activity by Toddlers and Caregivers*. Monographs of the Society for Research in Child Development, no. 58 (entire issue 7), 1993.

Wertsch, J. V., McNamee, G. D., McLane, J. G., and Budwig, N. A. "The Adult-Child Dyad as a Problem-Solving System." *Child Development*, 1980, 51, 1215–1221.

Wood, D. J., Bruner, J., and Ross, G. "The Role of Tutoring in Problem Solving." *Journal of Child Psychology and Psychiatry*, 1976, 17, 89–100.

This chapter presents and illustrates the theoretical position that as people participate in sociocultural activities, they contribute to the development of community practices that simultaneously contribute to the individuals' own development.

Development Through Participation in Sociocultural Activity

Barbara Rogoff, Jacqueline Baker-Sennett, Pilar Lacasa, Denise Goldsmith

In this chapter, we argue that development is a process of participation in sociocultural activities. We regard individual development as inseparable from interpersonal and community processes; individuals' changing roles are mutually defined with those of other people and with dynamic cultural processes. We make use of "activity" or "event" as the unit of analysis, with active and dynamic contributions from individuals, their social partners, and historical traditions and materials and their transformations (see Dewey and Bentley, 1949; Leontiev, 1981).

Studying human events or activities contrasts with the more traditional approach of examining the individual in isolation or in interaction with a separate environment. In our approach, individuals' efforts and sociocultural institutions and practices are constituted by and constitute each other and thus cannot be defined independently of each other or studied in isolation. We may focus on the contribution of one or another individual or a cultural tradition, but always in relation to the whole activity rather than extracted from it. When individuals participate in shared endeavors, not only does

We are grateful to the Spencer Foundation for its support of the research reported here; to the Ministerio de Educación y Ciencia de España for its support to Lacasa for her stay in the United States; to the troop leaders and Scouts who participated in the research; to Cindy White for her expert assistance; and to the personnel of the Girl Scouts of America, the Girl Scouts of Greater Philadelphia, the Cedar Hill Girl Scout Museum, and the cookie companies for their help with historical information. Cathy Angelillo, Pablo Chavajay, Eugene Matusov, and Cindy White provided helpful suggestions on a prior draft.

individual development occur, but the process transforms (develops) the practices of the community.

Community, interpersonal, and personal planes of analysis can each become the focus of a particular analysis, but without being separated from each other (Rogoff, in press b). Any given plane can be viewed in the foreground of a particular analysis while the others are maintained in the background. When we consider a single person's contributions or the functioning of a whole community in the foreground, we do not assume that they are separate elements or levels but rather planes of focus on the whole activity that facilitate analysis; all are essential to understand any of them.

Rogoff (in press b) describes the three analytic planes as follows. The *community plane of analysis* focuses on people participating with others in culturally organized activity, with institutional practices and development extending from historical events into the present, guided by cultural values and goals.

The *interpersonal plane of analysis* focuses on how people communicate and coordinate efforts in face-to-face and side-by-side interaction as well as more distal arrangements of people's activities—arrangements that do not require co-presence (for example, choices of where and with whom and with what materials and activities a person is involved). Interpersonal processes are not simply facilitative of involvement in certain activities but also include restriction of the activities in which people participate—for example, the exclusion of children from some adult activities or provision of messages that they are allowed to participate only in certain ways.

The *personal plane of analysis* focuses on how individuals change through their involvement in one or another activity, in the process becoming prepared for subsequent involvement in related activities. Through engagement in an activity at one time, individuals change and handle a later situation in ways prepared by their own participation in the previous situation. Studying the *process* of children's participation and changing responsibility in an activity is both how researchers can understand development and how development occurs.

We argue that development (whether viewed in the personal, interpersonal, or community plane) is a process of transformation through people's participation rather than of acquisition. We illustrate our argument using observations of the developmental processes of individual Girl Scouts and of community traditions of the Girl Scouts of America through the participation of individuals in the annual community cookie sale, an activity that allows us to examine personal, interpersonal, and community processes that we ourselves have not devised, facilitating analysis of the community plane in particular.

Explanation focusing on the community aspects of an activity requires reference to the personal and interpersonal aspects of the endeavor. Likewise, to understand personal or interpersonal processes, it is essential to understand the historical, institutional context of the activity, which both defines the practices of the individuals and their companions and is transformed by successive generations. In our example, individual Scouts are active in learning and in managing the activity, along with their companions, as they participate in and contribute to transforming community practices that began more than seven decades earlier.

We worked with two troops of ten- and eleven-year-old Scouts in Salt Lake City, Utah, in 1990. In one troop, we became "cookie chairs" and underwent the training to serve as the troop's organizers of the sale (a role usually filled by a mother of a girl in the troop, which one of us was). In the other troop, we observed the process. The girls suggested that we give them tape recorders to carry around to record their sales and deliveries; their tape recordings allowed us to observe changes in their roles and participation throughout the two-month process. In addition, we videotaped or audiotaped troop meetings and interviewed the girls throughout. We investigated the history of Girl Scout cookie sales with the help of individuals associated with the activity over a considerable time (including council historians, a Girl Scout museum curator, the director of Girl Scout cookie sales at the national level, and representatives from the official bakeries), public documents such as newspapers, and archives and publications of the Girl Scouts of America.

Development Viewed in the Community Plane

Research that focuses on development in the community plane examines transformations in the institutional structure and cultural technologies of the activity as a function of the generations of people who participate in the community. Community processes include not only formal institutions, such as schools and economic and political systems, but also informal systems of practices in which people participate. Berger and Luckmann (1966) speculate that habitual relations between people become institutionalized as expected and accepted rules and approaches that humans come to regard as external to their functioning. Shotter (1978) describes such institutional settings:

> For the structure of human exchanges, there are precise foundations to be discovered in the *institutions* we establish between ourselves and others; institutions which implicate us in one another's activity in such a way that, what we have done together in the past, *commits* us to going on in a certain way in the future. . . . The members of an institution need not necessarily have been its originators; they may be second, third, fourth, etc. generation members, having "inherited" the institution from their forebears. And this is a most important point, for although there may be an intentional structure to institutional activities, practitioners of institutional forms need have no awareness at all of the reason for its structure—for them, it is just "the-way-things-are-done." [p. 70]

Our aim in the first half of this chapter is to examine historical changes in the practice of Girl Scout cookie sales as the basis of our analysis of development in the community plane, with attention to how generations of Scouts and cookie companies have contributed to the ongoing, developing community processes constituting that practice. Analysis focusing on the community plane requires attention to the contributions of individuals and groups (the other two planes of analysis) as they participate in creating new traditions, by building on existing traditions and other communities and institutions. Because focusing on the community plane of analysis involves connecting not only with the personal and interpersonal planes of analysis but also with other communities and institutions, we examine both how the community practice of Girl Scout cookie sales has developed through the contributions of individuals and groups and how transformations in the practice relate to historical changes in other institutions (for example, family structure, maternal employment).

In the last half of the chapter, we shift focus to make a parallel argument: that the individual plane of analysis requires understanding the interpersonal and community planes of analysis. We hope to convince readers of the utility of thinking of developmental processes as involving personal, interpersonal, and community processes as they mutually constitute each other.

Personal and Interpersonal Contributions to Development of Community Practices. By 1990, when we conducted our study, cookie sales were the major annual fund-raising effort of the Girl Scouts of America, a voluntary organization dedicated to girls' moral education, development of home, academic, and outdoor skills, and career preparation (Kleinfeld and Shinkwin, 1983). The Scouts meet on a weekly basis in "troops" of about a dozen Scouts and one or two women leaders.[1] The funds from cookie sales are used to support the troops' activities, the regional administration, and girls' participation in camps run by the organization. In 1990, the average troop treasury cookie profit was $420 ("Girl Scouts Growing with Pride," 1991); nationwide revenues about this time period were $400 million (Zagorin, 1993).

The Scouts compose the sales force, trained and supervised by the organization, going door to door, selling to family, friends, and neighbors, and getting their parents to sell cookies at work. Most Scouts participate in the sales and take their economic role very seriously; their parents must sign a form agreeing to be responsible for the large sums of money involved. According to the *Christian Science Monitor* (Atkin, 1990), cookie sales are considered an educational tool to teach responsibility, goal-setting, and business principles.

Billboards and other advertisements remind potential customers of the tradition of buying Girl Scout cookies: "It's Girl Scout Cookie Time." Many Scouts have older sisters or mothers who themselves sold Girl Scout cookies when they were Scouts (three of the four authors of this chapter sold cookies as Scouts), and aged customers are often eager to buy cookies as they remember their own efforts to sell Girl Scout cookies. People who are not visited by a Scout selling cookies are often upset that they missed the chance to buy. According to the official publication of the Utah Girl Scout Council ("Growing with Pride," 1991), only 38 to 41 percent of the potential market is reached by the sales force.

Cookie sales and delivery occur with the constraints and resources provided by practices of the Girl Scouts of America and large baking companies licensed by the Girl Scouts, which set deadlines and provide organizational supports to the girls in their efforts to keep track of sales, cookies, and money and to manage their time and resources. The Scouts take orders on an order form provided by the cookie company and deliver cookies and collect money a month later, according to dates set by the regional administration. The layout of the order form is designed to facilitate calculation of amounts of money, presentation of information to customers, and the keeping track of deliveries. The order form is color-coded in a way that facilitates keeping track of the seven different kinds of cookies. (For example, customers order Thin Mints by indicating the number of boxes desired in the green column; the number of Trefoils is indicated in the yellow column. The boxes and cases of cookies and other materials maintain this color-coding.)

Today's elaborate system of color-coded order forms and sales training information evolved from a tiny form with a few printed suggestions for its use. An order form from the 1930s provided a stub for the purchaser to sign and a sticker for the purchaser to put in the window to give notice that the household had already purchased cookies. By 1951, in Newton, Massachusetts, the troop chair was supposed to meet with the girls a week before the cookie sale to "have a discussion of selling techniques and sales approaches" ("Annual Cookie Sale," 1951). By 1971, the brochure for the same area provided calculation information for the cookie chairs (1 box, $.60, 2 boxes, $1.20); in addition, the cookie chairs were to give selling aids and parent letters provided by the cookie company to each girl. Later in the 1970s, the order form for that area had a chart for orders with a checklist and a calculation box for the Scouts. It listed "Six Easy Lessons" on the back. By the time we conducted this study, ten tips, seven rules, and a letter of advice for parents were included on the back of the large, glossy, folded form that included a tear-off miniform for parents to post at their workplace.

In the troop in which we served as cookie chairs, we used the materials provided by the regional organization and the cookie companies to train Scouts to become "successful" salespeople: institutionally sanctioned sales pitches, information on how to use the color-coded order forms, rules related to safety when selling, and procedures for collecting money. The organizers also provided sales incentives and other materials for the cookie chairs, including a money-counting game that uses play money and a role-playing game in which troop members work in pairs, taking turns playing the parts of customer and salesperson.

According to the person from the Little Brownie Bakers (of Louisville, Ky.) in charge of cookie sales for the Utah area, a sales representative meets with the Girl Scout Council yearly to present any new ideas for the order form or type of cookies to be sold. The Council sometimes makes small suggestions about modifications, but this is rare. The cookie company does not make any effort to ensure that the form is manageable for young children; company officials believe that young children are so skilled in selling that few extra efforts need to be made to ensure that they will handle the task efficiently.

The role of individuals in the development of both Scouting and cookie sales is apparent in historical accounts of the origins of these traditions. Prominent women organized local Girl Scout organizations and assisted in the spread of Scouting, beginning with the first U.S. troop, which was founded in 1912 by Mrs. Juliette Low (who was inspired by a friend who had founded the Scout movement in England and by the English Girl Guides). Mrs. Low invited several girls to tea at her home in Savannah, Georgia, and explained the Scout movement; that group of girls was the first troop ("The Girl Scout Movement," 1932a; Wright, 1938). The contribution of those first Scouts to the tradition can be seen in the name of the organization, which changed from Girl Guides to Girl Scouts at the Scouts' request ("Girl Scouting as an Educational Movement," 1932b).

According to the Girl Scout Council Headquarters in New York (E. Christie, personal communication, 1991), cookie sales were first recognized in 1920, though they began on a small scale before then. The honors for originating the sales are claimed by various individuals and regional groups. The obituary for Bella Spewack, the Romanian-born co-writer of the Broadway musical *Kiss Me Kate,* reported that she had invented the Girl Scout cookie around 1922, when "she hit upon the now-familiar seal-embossed cookie as a promotional and money-making idea for Girl Scouts. She suggested that if the Scouts sold cookies at a flower show attended by actresses, the resulting publicity could launch national sales" (Oliver, 1990).

Each region seems to have its own "origin story" for the cookie sales. Wright's (1938) history of Girl Scouting in the Great Lakes region reported that the Chicago Girl Scouts held their first cookie contest and sale in 1923, using a national recipe to bake as well as sell the cookies, and that "the first trefoil-shaped cookie emerged from an Indianapolis oven, golden as a new-minted coin, which it proved to be! Since that first fragrant batch, annual cookie sales have furthered Girl Scouting over the entire United States. Like the house in Hänsel and Gretel, many a Girl Scout structure has been built out of cookies. In 1926, Detroit built a camp house and unit kitchens out of sixteen thousand dozen—$1,200!" (Wright, 1938, p. 34).

The archives of the Girl Scouts of Greater Philadelphia report that the first cookie sale was held in 1932 in the windows of the Philadelphia Gas and Electric Company. The Scouts were running baking demonstrations, and passersby asked to buy the freshly baked cookies. By 1934, 110,000 cookies baked in the shape of the Girl Scout trefoil insignia were made by a commercial Philadelphia baker for the sales (at 23 cents per box). In 1935, the sale was organized with a flyer and elaborate promotion plans, including notices in church calendars, radio and newspaper items, and announcements in neighborhood theaters in which Girl Scouts also sold cookies and served as ushers (Carhart, 1961).[2] The next year, cookie sales became a national event, and the national organization began franchising bakeries throughout the United States to make the cookies.

The fund-raising idea was so successful that by 1937 more than 125 regional councils had adopted it, according to S. Nowicki of the ABC "Official Girl Scout Cookie Bakers" (personal communication, June 1992). The Girl Scout council under whose auspices our Salt Lake troops worked began cookie sales in 1928; nationally endorsed sales began in 1936 (Lund, 1986).

In 1991, 7,500 Girl Scouts in Utah participated in cookie sales (Free, 1991) out of 10,307 Girl Scouts ("Membership Update," 1991); in 1990, Utah Girl Scouts sold an average of 179 boxes of cookies each—the highest average in the nation. The first-place seller in the Utah Girl Scout Council in 1991 sold 4,104 boxes, gaining membership in the 500-Cookie Club for her sixth year ("Looking Back," 1991). Nationally, 165 million boxes of cookies were sold in 1990 (Smith, 1991) by 1 million girls who were assisted officially by 400,000 adults (E. Christie, Girl Scout Council Headquarters, New York, personal communication, 1991).

Some of the transformations in the practice of cookie sales over the decades apparently derived from issues faced by individuals in the process, as is reported in the following account of the early Utah sales: "Cookies were ordered and when they arrived they were sold door to door and in shopping malls. Unfortunately, they occasionally miscalculated the number of boxes they could sell and a distraught cookie chairman was left with a garage full of cookies which she had to return to the manufacturer. This problem was remedied when they switched to pre-order sales in the 1950s" (Lund, 1986, p. 69).

From the historical accounts reported in this section we can see the role of individual contributions and of interpersonal contacts and efforts in the development and continual transformation of the tradition of Girl Scout cookie sales. Of course, the institutional context of Girl Scout cookie sales also relates to other institutions, such as cookie companies, family life, and the workplace, discussed below.

Involvement of Other Institutions in Girl Scout Cookie Sales. The unit of analysis to which we are referring in the community plane of analysis is not fixed; we could, for example, have referred to changing national events and practices in analyzing the community plane (as in Elder and Caspi, 1988). The focus of a particular plane can broaden or widen according to the analysis; it is not an operational definition. We consider people to be members of a variety of interrelated communities (which may be commonly defined in terms of their family membership, religious involvement, occupational or gender organization, ethnic involvement, and so on).

From its early days, the Girl Scout movement had obvious relations to other institutions, including the Scouting movement in England and the Boy Scouts of America. In addition, some of the adults facilitating the early growth of Scouting, such as Mrs. Herbert Hoover and Jane Addams of Chicago (Wright, 1938), were active in other important political, educational, and social-welfare organizations.

A 1932 Girl Scout publication ("Girl Scouting as an Educational Movement," 1932b) noted the relation of the Girl Scout educational philosophy to educational movements and institutions of the time. The following passage from that publication beautifully indicates the historical links between the activities of Scouting (including cookie sales) and those of other community institutions:

> Fundamentally, the educational principles of Girl Scouting are those underlying all progressive educational thinking and progressive educational experiments [for example, the educational philosophy of Dewey]. . . . They are being put into practice with all the resources of modern psychology and modern social and scientific theory.
>
> Girl Scouting believes that education is life, not merely preparation for life—in other words, that living the present fully, intelligently, and wholeheartedly at any stage of development is the only true preparation for living later stages. It begins, therefore, with the interests and enthusiasms of a particular group of girls and provides a series of experiences which widen and enrich these interests and enthusiasms.
>
> Girl Scouting believes in the immense educational value of the small group, managing its own affairs and making its own plans as far as possible and learning in this way the first lessons of cooperation and good citizenship.
>
> The Girl Scout leader is a friend and guide of her girls, rather than a grown person in absolute authority. She makes suggestions as a member of the group, but respects the girls' proposals and ideas. [pp. 3–4]

Links with other community institutions are apparent in the impact of the structure of family and neighborhood life in the United States on the organization of Girl Scout cookie sales. Stresses in family stability (for example, the increase in divorce) and mothers' role changes have changed the supports available at home for children's endeavors. In addition, the prevalence of women working outside the home has led to changes in the way the sales occur. Decades ago, Scouts could count on finding customers at home throughout the day; now they have to return many times to find their customers at home or limit deliveries to evenings and weekends. It is also regarded as less safe for girls to go door to door in their neighborhoods now than in previous eras.

These changes may have contributed to the development of greater reliance on parents selling in the workplace. Some zealous parents use fax machines to take orders. One mother sent out an e-mail message to co-workers at her company, seeking orders (saying, "I don't have the luxury of taking her out to sell cookies," Smith, 1991, p. L3). She had sold about sixty boxes when two Girl Scout fathers—influential people in the company who until that year had dominated the office cookie sales—took her aside and pointed out that she had started before the official start date for sales. The company's personnel office then worked out a way for employees to pool their cookie orders and divide the proceeds evenly.

According to Smith (1991, p. L3), "Girl Scout officials say that . . . changing families and neighborhoods have altered the sweetest of U.S. institutions.

'Long ago, the streets were safer and the little girls used to go around in neighborhoods. Those were the halcyon days when everybody was home,' said Cece Sander, director of product sales for the Orange County council. Now an increasing number of Girl Scouts are in single-parent homes. 'The workplace has become in many cases a substitute for the prior activity. One, it's safer, and two, it's more effective,' Sander said."

It is not just the parents who are transforming sales practices to make use of current technologies (such as the fax and e-mail) and institutions (such as the company organization). Over the years, older Scouts have found themselves at a disadvantage in door-to-door sales as the sales force has changed to include younger Scouts, who have the personal resource of being "cute" and therefore more successful in the neighborhood sales. In 1989, the San Gorgonio Council instituted a toll-free phone number for customers to place orders directly; older Girl Scouts packaged the orders for delivery by United Parcel Service, yielding a 28 percent surge in orders. In 1990, the Girl Scout Council in Los Angeles began teaching older Scouts to function as sophisticated telemarketers (LaGanga, 1990).

This section has focused on the evolution of community practices, with reference to the contributions of individuals and groups as well as to connections with other societal changes. Understanding the processes that become the focus in personal, interpersonal, and community/institutional planes of analysis relies on understanding the processes in the background as well as those in the foreground of analysis.

Development Viewed in the Personal Plane

In this section, we consider how a participation perspective leads to different assumptions and questions about the processes of development. We provide a conceptual analysis of development as a process of participation rather than of acquisition and illustrate our points with observations of the Scouts and accounts of several individuals for whom this year's sale was their first. Our dual aim is to show how an analysis of individual development requires reference to other planes of analysis and to examine changes in how we conceive of development from a participation perspective.

Individuals transform their understanding of and responsibility for activities through their own participation, and in the process they become prepared to engage in similar subsequent activities. By functioning in an activity, participating in its meaning, people necessarily make ongoing contributions, whether in concrete actions or in stretching to understand the actions and ideas of others. Communication and coordination in the course of participation in shared endeavors involve adjustments between participants (with varying, not necessarily compatible roles) to stretch their common understanding to fit with new perspectives in the shared endeavor. Such stretching to accomplish something together during participation in activities is development. As Wertsch and Stone (1979, p. 21) put it, "The process *is* the product." No particular event is privileged as the "outcome" (see Rogoff, Radziszewska, and Masiello, in press). In Dewey's words, "The living creature is a part of the world, sharing its vicissitudes and fortunes, and making itself secure in its precarious dependence only as it intellectually identifies itself with the changes about it, and, forecasting the future consequences of what is going on, shapes its own activities accordingly. If the living, experiencing being is an intimate participant in the activities of the world to which it belongs, then knowledge is a mode of participation, valuable in the degree in which it is effective. It cannot be the idle view of an unconcerned spectator" (1916, p. 393).

Children and their social partners are interdependent; their roles are active and dynamically change in activities of the community. In Girl Scout cookie sales, individuals learn to solve complex problems that have been defined and organized by their community; their own changes in roles and understanding extend to their efforts and involvements on similar occasions in the future and simultaneously contribute to transformation of the activities in which they participate.

For example, in our observations, the girls began to use and extend cultural tools for calculating and keeping track of amounts due from customers that tied their efforts in this activity to practices in other institutions of their culture, including the number system used in their community and the calculation box on the order form provided by the organization. Their means of handling the problems of sales and delivery involved using various tools developed in the process and borrowed from others. In organizing the individual orders, the girls often bundled together the boxes for each order using a technique that in some cases we could track as being borrowed from other Scouts or from mothers (for example, putting a rubber band around the boxes and labeling the bundle with a Post-it adhesive note with the customer's address and the amount due). In calculating amounts due, the girls had available to them their mothers' help in talking them through the calculations for many orders and the model of their customers' talk-aloud calculation at the time of the sale (while the customers filled out the order form) that demonstrated how calculations on a unit price of $2.50 could be handled by thinking of a box costing a fourth of $10 rather than by multiplying out each digit.

Viewing development as participation challenges the idea of a boundary between internal and external phenomena (for example, between arithmetic knowledge and availability of order forms listing price information)—a boundary that is derived from use of the isolated individual as the unit of analysis. A person is a part of an activity in which he or she participates, not separate from it. Our perspective discards the idea that the social world is external to the individual and that development consists of *acquiring* knowledge and skills. Rather, a person develops through participation in an activity, changing to be involved in the situation at hand in ways that contribute both to the ongoing event and to the person's preparation for involvement in other, similar events.

If development is seen as a process of transformation of responsibilities and understanding, as we suggest, cognition need not be defined as a collection of stored possessions (such as representations of spatial routes or plans for making deliveries). Instead of studying a person's possession or acquisition of a capacity or a bit of knowledge, the focus is on the active changes involved in an unfolding event or activity in which people participate (see Gibson, 1979; Leontiev, 1981; Meacham, 1984; Pepper, 1942; Rogoff, 1990; Rogoff, Baker-Sennett, and Matusov, in press).

The Scouts' participation in cookie sales and delivery inherently involves planning and adjusting their approaches as they learn to manage the complex planning involved in developing spatial routes with sufficient flexibility to be efficient given the interpersonal and material resources and constraints of the situation (for example, customers that are not home, routes that require revision, helpers that wear out). Flexibility in planning—rather than possession of a plan independent of action—is paramount, with a planner observing the changing circumstances, ready to adjust plans or take advantage of an opportunity (Rogoff, Baker-Sennett, and Matusov, in press).

While planning, a person necessarily coordinates his or her efforts with those of others, while anticipating and building on opportunities and barriers to their efforts that involve events requiring analysis in the interpersonal and community planes as well as the individual plane of analysis.

The focus in a participation model of development thus turns to how planning, remembering, relating to others, and so on involve participation in cultural practices with other people (even when a person is alone for a while). Change and development in the process of participation are assumed to be inherent.

An important difference between viewing development as a matter of transformation and viewing it as a matter of acquisition is in assumptions about time. The notion of acquisition rests on the assumption that time is segmented into past, present, and future, which are treated as separate. This yields problems of accounting for relations across time—problems that are often handled by assuming that the individual stores memories of the past, which are somehow retrieved and used in the present, and that the individual makes plans in the present and (if the plans are stored effectively) executes them in the future. The links between these separate time segments are bridged in mysterious ways, to bring information or skills stored at one point in time to use in another. The acquisition view of development involves a storage model of mind—with elements stored in the brain that requires a homunculus or difficult-to-specify executive process to bring the elements stored at one epoch to implement at another epoch (Rogoff, Baker-Sennett, and Matusov, in press). This is the same mysterious executive process that is required to bring external pieces of knowledge or skill inside the person if learning is seen as the acquisition and accumulation of objects stored in the brain.

From our perspective, on the other hand, time is an inherent aspect of events and is not divided into separate units of past, present, and future (see Rogoff, in press b). Any event in the present is an extension of previous events and is directed toward goals that have not yet been accomplished. As such, the present extends through the past and future and cannot be separated from them. When a person acts on the basis of previous experience, that person's past is present. It is not merely a stored memory called up in the present; the person's previous participation contributes to the event at hand by having prepared it. The present event is different than it would have been if previous events had not occurred. This explanation does not require a storage model of past events.

An analogy illustrating the superfluousness of a storage model of past events can be drawn from the way we conceive of organizational change. Changes in the structure of Girl Scout cookie sales, for example, are not stored anywhere as accumulated units of some kind; they are built on the efforts of previous years in ways that prepare current and future practices. Both continuity and change are inherent in activities. Therefore it appears to us more parsimonious to examine the changes and continuities in the activities themselves than to add a construct of storage.

In our view, development is a dynamic process characterized by change throughout rather than the accumulation of new items. There is no need to conceive of development in terms of the acquisition or transmission of stored units, since development through participation is an aspect of ongoing events (see also Rogoff, in press *a*). People change through their participation and handle subsequent events in ways prepared by their changes in previous events.

From the perspective that development occurs through participation, it follows that personal, interpersonal, and cultural processes all constitute each other and develop in sociocultural activity. This contrasts with a model that casts development as acquisition, in which one looks first for exposure to external knowledge or skill and then for evidence of acquisition as the person retrieves the acquired knowledge or skill independently (Rogoff, Radziszewska, and Masiello, in press). In such a model, the individual would be viewed as either a passive recipient of external social or cultural influence—a receptacle for the accumulation of knowledge and skill—or an active seeker of passive external social and cultural knowledge and skill.

The questions to investigate are different if we move from seeing development as acquisition to viewing development as a process of transformation through participation in sociocultural activities. Questions of where memories are stored or how information is taken from external events or how children accumulate knowledge or implement plans all become less relevant ways to study development from this sociocultural approach. (Rogoff, Baker-Sennett, and Matusov [in press] do not argue for necessarily dropping the stored mental representation metaphor but for recognizing it *as a metaphor,* one perhaps useful for communication between scholars but not to be assumed to characterize the functioning of the people studied. Greater clarity may result if the metaphor is dropped for some research questions.)

From a participation perspective, we begin to examine in closer focus the actual processes by which children participate with other people in cultural activity and the ways they transform their participation. The investigation of people's involvement in activities becomes the basis of our understanding of development rather than simply the surface that we try to get past. The central question becomes how people participate in sociocultural activity and how their participation changes from a relatively peripheral involvement, observing and carrying out secondary roles, to assuming various responsible roles in the management of such activities. As Lave and Wenger (1991) note, "Viewing learning as legitimate peripheral participation means that learning is not merely a condition for membership, but is itself an evolving form of membership. We conceive of identities as long term, living relations between persons and their place and participation in communities of practice. Thus identity, knowing, and social membership entail one another" (p. 53).

The transformations are developmental in the sense that they are changes in particular directions. The direction of development varies locally (in accordance with cultural values, interpersonal needs, and specific circumstances); it does not require specification of universal or ideal endpoints. In addition, the applicability of these ideas is not restricted to activities and development that are considered desirable by experts or other segments of the community. They apply equally to explaining how people develop through participation in community activities that many would criticize.

Given our emphasis on development as changing forms of participation, key questions for developmental research are these: How do the activity, its purpose, and people's roles in it transform as it proceeds? How do different activities relate to each other and to prior events? How do people prepare now for what they expect may happen later? How do the activities of previous generations prepare the current situation? We would want to know the following:

What roles people play, with what fidelity and responsibility

Their changing purposes for being involved, commitment to the endeavor, and trust of unknown aspects of it (including its future)

Their flexibility and attitude toward change in involvement (that is, their interest in learning versus their rejection of new roles or protection of the status quo)

Their understanding of the interrelations of different contributions to the endeavor and their readiness to switch to complementary roles (for example, to fill in for others)

The relation of their roles in this activity to those in other activities (such as the relation between participation in roles at school and at home or their involvement in several different ethnic communities)

How their involvement relates to changes in the community's practices.

Orienting our inquiry by focusing on how people participate in sociocultural activity and how they change their participation demystifies the processes of learning and development. Rather than searching for the mechanisms of acquisition or the nature of internalization as a conduit from external bits of knowledge or skill to an internal repository, to see development we look directly at children's efforts and the efforts of their companions and the institutions that they constitute and upon which they build.

In the study of Girl Scout cookie sales and delivery, we were able to observe changes in how the girls participated in a number of aspects of the activity and how, through participation, they *developed* in responsibility and understanding of the practice. One purpose of our account, as we have noted, is to illustrate how a focus on the developmental process of individuals requires reference to (not separation from) their involvement with others and the traditions of the community (in the other two planes of analysis). We focus here on the development of the girls through their participation in this activity; similar analyses could be done of the development of the troop leaders, family members, customers, and researchers through their participation in the activity.

The girls, as well as their social partners, actively borrowed and developed one or another approach and made use of available resources; they also negotiated a balance of responsibility for shared efforts. For example, in the calculation of charges to customers, we could track in many cases how the girls took on greater responsibility over the course of the delivery, with their mothers often initially managing the calculations and supervising the girls in keeping track of customers who had paid; in the course of participation in a system that was often set up by the mothers, the girls took on greater responsibility for handling these complicated and important aspects of the activity.

Our observations revealed developmental processes that occurred as the girls participated in this sociocultural activity. Through the girls' participation in the activity, they developed in ways that we could see leading to changed later participation. To support these points, we describe the changing roles and forms of participation of the four Scouts in our study (two from each troop) for whom this year's sale was the first.

Learning and Changing Roles in Becoming a Seller. We observed that the process of participation in cookie sales involved changes in the girls' roles as they became salespersons—changes that were apparent in their treatment of their own roles over the course of the activity. We hope that readers will notice that our account of the developmental changes for the girls as salespersons involves not only a focus on their own efforts and transformations (in the personal plane of analysis) but also necessary reference to their involvement with other people (in the interpersonal plane of analysis) and the traditions of the practice (in the community plane of analysis).

The process of becoming cookie sellers had both commonalities and important differences from girl to girl. The commonalities had to do with transformations in their confidence and their growing identity as cookie sellers who coordinated with the community practices of cookie sales. Some of the differences had to do with the kind of support offered by other people and the roles of the other people. The family circumstances of the girls were quite different, and these differences seemed to relate to variations in their adoption of the main responsibility for the role of seller. All the girls marshaled or were offered support by others in making the transformation: one struggled with the primary responsibility herself, two collaborated with others who provided a great deal of support, and one remained somewhat peripheral to the process as organized in her family. The people supporting their transformation varied, with major aid coming in different cases from troop leaders, customers, other Girl Scouts, parents, and siblings.

Thus the girls transformed in their roles as Girl Scout cookie sellers, and they did so with the assistance of others as they came to participate in the tradition of cookie sales (which, by their participation, they contributed to creating). Understanding the Scouts' changing roles requires attention not only to their own efforts but to their coordination with and guidance from others and from the organization of the activity (through the materials and practices developed over the decades by prior Scouts, adult leaders, and customers) and through the changes in other institutions (such as family structure).

Darlene. Darlene's parents were divorced, and she spent much of her after-school time at home by herself. Darlene treated the sales as primarily her responsibility and asked many anxious questions regarding potential problems at troop meetings. Her struggles to manage the sales and delivery illustrate the necessity of considering the interpersonal and community planes of analysis in understanding how a person develops as a cookie seller.

At first, Darlene had many difficulties with implementation of the sales script. For example, although she had been instructed not to collect money from customers until the cookies were delivered, she collected some money during the sales period. As she explained to one of the cookie chairs in requesting clarification of the procedure, "Well, I've been kind of collecting some money now. . . . A lot of [customers] just shove it in your face and slam the door." Darlene's troop leader and the cookie chairs took on several roles related to Darlene's participation that were ordinarily filled by the girls' mothers (such as picking up the cases of cookies from the cookie chair).

Over Darlene's six different sales trips (the first five of which were done without a companion), there was a noticeable change in her comfort with the role of salesperson. Her transition in skill and identity as a salesperson was supported not only by the script suggested on the order form and the training provided by the cookie chairs but also by the customers. The script on the order form provided specific wordings for the girls to introduce themselves, explain what they were doing, and take the order, along with suggestions for successful sales. The training provided in the role-playing game suggested by the regional Girl Scout organization gave Darlene and the other Scouts the opportunity to practice the complementary roles of seller and customer during a troop meeting.

Nonetheless, during her first sale, Darlene struggled with the identity of a cookie seller as she approached a neighbor: "I was wondering. . . . What you're *supposed* to say is, 'My name is Darlene. I'm from Troop 23, and we're selling Girl Scout cookies.'" Assuming the role and the language of a salesperson was not yet comfortable for Darlene. However, the neighbor was sympathetic and suggested that Darlene return to sell to her roommates. When Darlene returned, the neighbor encouraged her to practice her sales pitch on each roommate. Darlene later practiced her sales pitch on her father and stepmother as well; they pretended to be ordinary customers, with her father refusing to buy and her stepmother encouraging Darlene to provide information on each type of cookie (and commenting, after they bought three boxes, "We're just very impressed. I've never had a salesgirl quite that good"). Another customer, who said she "used to do this," helped Darlene use the form properly, telling her that customers should fill out the form with the number of boxes they want, not just use checks.

As the sales progressed, Darlene became a skilled seller, effectively communicating knowledge of her product, using the order form effectively, and adjusting her sales pitch and interpersonal manner to fit each customer. However, Darlene also had difficulties managing the complexities of cookie delivery with little assistance: she collected too much money for the number of cookies sold.

Carla. Carla, unlike Darlene, depended heavily on the leadership of family members. Either her sister or her mother or both were with her at all times; her mother called friends throughout the sales to let them know that Carla was selling Girl Scout cookies, gave Carla ideas about where to sell, and routinely checked the order form throughout the sales phase to make sure that amounts due were tallied correctly. Carla did not regard herself as the person responsible for selling. On one occasion, she told her sister to knock on a customer's door, saying, "I don't understand why I always have to do it."

When we asked how she had delivered the cookies, Carla's response made it clear that her mother had organized most of the delivery from the time they picked up their cases of cookies from the cookie chair: "My mom took all of the boxes and we stuck them in the front room and then Mom went through them. . . . First my mom called everybody . . . and then we went to their houses. . . . She wrote down everybody's name . . . and then she stuck the cookies and the piece of paper with their names and how many they ordered and how much money [in a plastic bag]." Carla's mother was with her for every delivery except one to help keep track of the money; this may have contributed to the fact that Carla was one of the first girls in the troop to turn in all her money.

Lorna. Lorna was assisted in becoming a cookie seller by her friend Elaine, a more experienced seller from the same troop whom Lorna treated as an expert. Lorna, like Darlene, seemed unsure of herself at the beginning of the first sales trip; she asked Elaine to do the speaking at the first house, for example. At first Lorna resisted Elaine's idea that they separate to visit different houses, protesting, "I don't know." After they went to one house together, Lorna agreed with Elaine's suggestion that the two girls go to different houses and then meet up; by the third stop, Lorna was the one proposing that they go to different houses; and after about ten stops, Lorna was proposing the specific route, although this was Elaine's and not Lorna's neighborhood.

Amy. Amy, like Lorna, began her sales with the support of an experienced Scout from her troop. On her first selling trip, Amy went with Sue to keep her company and learn a little about how to sell; she made no sales of her own. On that trip, Sue gave several tips to Amy, worded in ways that made her advisory role clear (for example, "I'd advise you one thing . . ."). Sue explained to Amy how to approach customers and how to use the order form to facilitate calculations:

SUE: Well, what you do is, you know how it's two-fifty a box?

AMY: I guess.

SUE: Well, it's two-fifty a box. So what you do is, it helps to fill this out [the box in the corner of the order form with blanks for prices for different numbers of boxes], if it doesn't take too much time. Write two-fifty, and then for two boxes it's five dollars, . . .

AMY: Mmm hmm.

SUE: Three boxes seven-fifty, four boxes ten dollars, and so on. . . . You just fill that out. So what you do is they [the customers] just add up. [We can see from Amy's order form that she followed this advice and wrote in the prices.] . . . And then they put how much it is right here.

In her first sale after her practice trip with her friend, Amy spoke with confidence as a seller: "I was wondering if you would like to buy any Girl Scout cookies." Nonetheless, she still had difficulty with some aspects of the sales procedure, including not having the customers fill out the order form themselves. The customers assisted her in solving some problems: "Okay. Let's see, you put that in the wrong thing. Should I cross that out? . . . You didn't put anything down on our line." Amy acknowledged this correction, "Okay, thanks."

Conclusions Regarding Development Through Participation and Three Planes of Analysis

We hope that it is apparent in our account of these four cases that these Scouts, new to cookie selling, changed in the process of their participation with others to become sellers, dealing with issues of planning, calculation, keeping track of progress, and managing the seller's role in ways that fit with the sociocultural organization apparent in their particular circumstances. We want to emphasize three points regarding the girls' development:

• The girls' development cannot be explained in terms that would isolate them from the contributions of other people and of the traditions of the practice in which they were participating; focusing on the personal plane of analysis requires background analyses of the interpersonal and community planes of analysis.

• Rather than seeing the girls' development in terms of acquisition of skills (plans, mathematical heuristics, and so on), we regard the process as one of personal transformation, with changes in how an endeavor is handled as a function of the girls' participation in the activity. As Lave and Wenger (1991) argue, learning and identity are inseparable aspects of the same phenomenon: "Learning thus implies becoming a different person with respect to the possibilities enabled by these systems of relations. To ignore this aspect of learning is to overlook the fact that learning involves the construction of identities" (p. 53).

• The girls' participation in the meaning of shared endeavors varied regarding the nature of their engagement. It did not necessarily involve symmetrical (that is, equal) relations and often did not entail direct joint action with others in the activity. A person who is actively observing and following the decisions made by another is participating whether or not he or she contributes directly to the decisions as they are made. And a person who is for a time acting alone is also engaged in sociocultural activity as he or she follows and builds on community traditions for the activity. All four girls participated in the activity of selling cookies, with undoubtedly differing preparation for future selling as a result of the roles that they played.

The importance of learning through varying roles, especially peripheral involvement and observation, which have often been overlooked, have been emphasized by Lave and Wenger (1991), Rogoff, Mistry, Göncü, and Mosier (1993), Heath (1983), and Ward (1971). New members of a community are active in their attempts to make sense of activities and may be primarily responsible for putting themselves in a position to participate. Communication and coordination with other members of the community stretch the understanding of all participants as they seek a common ground of understanding n order to proceed with the activities at hand. The search for a common grou d, as well as extensions from it, involves adjustments and growth of underst nding.

Elabo ting on White and Siegel's (1984) notion that child development consists of articipation in widening contexts of the community, we argue that children pa icipate in a number of different communities, such as those represented by heir ethnic groups, school, neighborhood, extended family, gender group, nd religious and other affiliations. How people integrate (or struggle to integrate) their roles, knowledge, and identities across different communities entails an active process of coming to participate more fully in overlapping and/or conflicting communities. For example, Carla (and her mother) sold to "church people"; thus Carla's selling involved coordinating her roles in the communities of Scouting, church, and family life. The juxtaposition of roles in different communities was apparent for the girls; for example, their leadership roles in selling cookies and their junior roles in relating with church members overlapped and sometimes came into conflict. Adjustments in responsibilities—learning to manage *differing* expectations, identities, and roles—are an inherent aspect of development, and they also provide researchers with a window on the classic issues of transfer of learning and change and continuity across situations.

This account of the Girl Scouts' activity illustrates how understanding both the development of individual Scouts and that of the practice of Girl Scout cookie sales requires understanding personal, interpersonal, and community planes of analysis together. The girls and their companions participated in and contributed to intellectual and economic institutions and traditions of their society and the Scout organization with associated cultural values (such as efficiency, persuasion of others within societal bounds of propriety, competition for achievement, and responsible completion of agreed-upon tasks).

The efforts of generations of individuals and their historically changing institutions form what we study in the community plane of analysis. This is the basis for our perspective that development (of individuals, groups, and the community alike) occurs with people's changing participation in sociocultural activities.

Notes

1. We write of the situation in 1990 in the present tense, though practices continue to evolve, of course, and some features will have changed by the time you read this.
2. Promotions continue. A kickoff in 1990 included a cookie sculpture contest for leading Boston hotels and bakeries, won by the Westin Hotel for its rendition of the Boston Public Gardens, made with 27,684 cookies (Atkin, 1990).

References

"Annual Cookie Sale." Newton, Mass.: Newton Local Council of the Girl Scouts, 1951.

Atkin, R. "As American as Girl Scout Cookies." *Christian Science Monitor,* Mar. 26, 1990.

Berger, P. L., and Luckmann, T. *The Social Construction of Reality.* New York: Doubleday, 1966.

Carhart, M. L. Interoffice memo re: history of cookie sale, Mar. 1961. (Available from Eileen Honert, archivist, Girl Scouts of Greater Philadelphia, Inc.)

Dewey, J. *Democracy and Education.* New York: Macmillan, 1916.

Dewey, J., and Bentley, A. F. *Knowing and the Known.* Boston: Beacon Press, 1949.

Elder, G. H., Jr., and Caspi, A. "Human Development and Social Change: An Emerging Perspective on the Life Course." In N. Bolger, A. Caspi, G. Downey, and M. Moorehouse (eds.), *Persons in Context: Developmental Processes.* New York: Cambridge University Press, 1988.

"Everybody's Pulling for the '71 Cookie Sale." Newton, Mass.: Newton Local Council of the Girl Scouts, 1971.

Free, C. "Girl Scout's Cookies as Irresistible as Sales Pitch." *Salt Lake Tribune,* Feb. 25, 1991, p. B1.

Gibson, J. J. *The Ecological Approach to Visual Perception.* Boston: Houghton Mifflin, 1979.

"Girl Scout Cookies and How to Sell Them." Lowell, Mass.: Megowen Educator Food Company, 1951.

"Girl Scout Movement, The." New York: Girl Scouts, Inc., 1932a.

"Girl Scouting as an Educational Movement." New York: Girl Scouts, Inc., 1932b.

"Girl Scouts Growing with Pride: 1991 Cookie Sale Parent Information Booklet." Salt Lake City: Utah Girl Scout Council, 1991.

"Growing with Pride: 1991 Cookie Campaign." *Trooper,* Jan. 1991, p. 6.

Heath, S. B. *Ways with Words: Language, Life, and Work in Communities and Classrooms.* New York: Cambridge University Press, 1983.

Kleinfeld, J., and Shinkwin, A. "Lessons Out of School: Boy Scouts, Girl Scouts, and 4-H

Clubs as Educational Environments." Paper presented at the meeting of the American Educational Research Association, Montreal, Apr. 13, 1983.

LaGanga, M. L. "Your Number Will Soon Be Up in Girl Scout Cookie Sale." *Los Angeles Times,* Mar. 2, 1990, pp. A1, A18.

Lave, J., and Wenger, E. *Situated Learning: Legitimate Peripheral Participation.* New York: Cambridge University Press, 1991.

Leontiev, A. N. "The Problem of Activity in Psychology." In J. V. Wertsch (ed.), *The Concept of Activity in Soviet Psychology.* Armonk, N.Y.: Sharpe, 1981.

"Looking Back: Celebrating Accomplishments of 1990–91." *Trooper,* Fall 1991, p. 4.

Lund, J. "The Girl Scouts in Utah: An Administrative History 1921–1985." Unpublished master's thesis, Brigham Young University, 1986.

Meacham, J. A. "The Social Basis of Intentional Action." *Human Development,* 1984, 27, 119–124.

"Membership Update." *Trooper,* Spring 1991, p. 3.

Oliver, M. "Bella Spewack: Writer, Scout Cookie Inventor." *Los Angeles Times,* Apr. 29, 1990, p. A40.

Pepper, S. C. *World Hypotheses: A Study in Evidence.* Berkeley: University of California Press, 1942.

Rogoff, B. *Apprenticeship in Thinking: Cognitive Development in Social Context.* New York: Oxford University Press, 1990.

Rogoff, B. "Developmental Transitions in Children's Participation in Sociocultural Activities." In A. Sameroff and M. Haith (eds.), *Reason and Responsibility: The Passage Through Childhood.* Chicago: University of Chicago Press, in press a.

Rogoff, B. "Observing Sociocultural Activity in Three Planes: Participatory Appropriation, Guided Participation, Apprenticeship." In A. Alvarez, P. del Rio, and J. V. Wertsch (eds.), *Perspectives on Sociocultural Research.* New York: Cambridge University Press, in press b.

Rogoff, B., Baker-Sennett, J., and Matusov, E. "Considering the Concept of Planning." In M. Haith, J. Benson, B. Pennington, and R. Roberts (eds.), *Future-Oriented Processes.* Chicago: University of Chicago Press, in press.

Rogoff, B., Mistry, J. J., Göncü, A., and Mosier, C. *Guided Participation in Cultural Activity by Toddlers and Caregivers.* Monographs of the Society for Research in Child Development, no. 58 (entire issue 7), 1993.

Rogoff, B., Radziszewska, B., and Masiello, T. "The Analysis of Developmental Processes in Sociocultural Activity." In L. Martin, K. Nelson, and E. Tobach (eds.), *Cultural Psychology and Activity Theory.* New York: Cambridge University Press, in press.

Shotter, J. "The Cultural Context of Communication Studies: Theoretical and Methodological Issues." In A. Lock (ed.), *Action, Gesture, and Symbol: The Emergence of Language.* San Diego, Calif.: Academic Press, 1978.

Smith, L. "How the Cookie Crumbles: Girl Scout Sales Become Office Politics." *Oregonian,* Feb. 10, 1991, p. L3.

Ward, M. C. *Them Children: A Study in Language Learning.* Troy, Mo.: Holt, Rinehart & Winston, 1971.

Wertsch, J. V., and Stone, C. A. "A Social Interactional Analysis of Learning Disabilities Remediation." Paper presented at the International Conference of the Association for Children with Learning Disabilities, San Francisco, Feb. 1979.

White, S. H., and Siegel, A. W. "Cognitive Development in Time and Space." In B. Rogoff and J. Lave (eds.), *Everyday Cognition: Its Development in Social Context.* Cambridge, Mass.: Harvard University Press, 1984.

Wright, K. O. *Girl Scouting in the Great Lakes Region: A History.* Chicago: Girl Scouts, Inc., 1938.

Zagorin, A. "Remember the Greedy." *Time,* Aug. 16, 1993, pp. 36–38.

BARBARA ROGOFF *is professor of psychology at the University of California, Santa Cruz.*

JACQUELINE BAKER-SENNETT *is assistant professor of educational psychology and special education, University of British Columbia, Vancouver.*

PILAR LACASA *is professor of psychology, Universidad Nacional de Educación a Distancia, Madrid.*

DENISE GOLDSMITH *is doing child clinical work in Salt Lake City, Utah.*

Editors' Preface to "Precepts and Practices"

The essence of Barbara Miller's study is its attention to the ways in which competing cultural viewpoints, competing possible identities, are played out in practice. Before we look at its more specific features, however, let us set the stage more broadly. The topic combines two proposals often found within analyses of development-in-context. The first comes predominantly from general analyses of culture—analyses that emphasize the presence of multiple perspectives that often compete with one another and change in their dominance over one another. The second proposal comes predominantly from developmental studies directed toward individuals who are often seen as faced with the task of "navigating the borders" (Phelan, Davidson, and Caro, in press) of home and school, of mainstream and minority cultures, or of old and new national cultures.

One of the basic tenets in descriptions of cultural contexts is that cultures usually contain more than one view of the world, more than one way of doing things (see Miller and Goodnow, this volume). This view of culture helps account for the ease with which people may shift quickly from one viewpoint to another. Both viewpoints are within their repertoire; what changes is the salience or the degree of endorsement given to one rather than to another (Quinn and Holland, 1987). This view of culture also helps account for what may appear to be inconsistency. Many parents, for example, believe that allowance money and children's household jobs should be "completely separate." At the same time, however, they subscribe to a second widespread view: "If [children] are getting money, they should do something in return; nothing is for nothing." Unless we recognize the presence of both viewpoints, Goodnow and Warton (1992) argue, it is difficult to account for the practices that most parents follow and the variety of positions they endorse in questionnaires.

To any listing of the alternatives that a culture contains (and that individuals absorb), however, we need to add this question: How are these alternatives played out? Suppose we accept the notion that cultural contexts contain competing models of the world. How is a challenge to one or another model made, interpreted, or met? At the level of social change, that is the kind of question Foucault (1980) takes up in his analysis of "alternative" medicine or education. People turn to alternatives, he argues, when they become discontented with what the dominant practices or viewpoints have to offer; the shift becomes a way of criticizing the dominant view. If the criticism becomes widespread, the practitioners of the dominant view then move to absorb the alternatives as part of their own practices.

When we turn to individual development, traditional Western theory directs our attention to adolescence as the period of life associated with the freedom to explore the multiple perspectives available in one's society, a time for sorting through values and life options en route to forging a meaningful identity (Erikson, 1968). For those who are torn between two social worlds, however, the choices may seem severely limited or even rigged, with "options" carrying with them threats to identity.

For example, in minority groups with a history of subjugation and continued economic discrimination, some teenagers embrace an "oppositional identity" in which values associated with the white majority are rejected; others chart a course of upward mobility, often with considerable risk to their sense of belonging to their own ethnic group (Ogbu, 1990). Burton, Obeidallah, and Allison (in press) describe African-American teenagers growing up in poverty who, in the course of a single day, might protect a younger sister from hostile peers, nurse a dying grandmother, and deal drugs on the street. The multiple pressures on these young people and the early age at which they assume adult responsibilities lead Burton to question whether the notion of adolescence—as an extended transition or moratorium—applies.

The bicultural group on which Barbara Miller focuses is one whose history and current circumstances contrast sharply with those studied by Ogbu and Burton. She studies the sons and daughters of Hindu immigrants who came to the United States voluntarily. Most of the parents are highly educated and well-to-do, and ethnic prejudice declines as the children move through the educational system. Yet even under these largely favorable conditions, adolescents, especially girls, experience the pressure of dual expectations from parents and peers.

Miller turns to practices such as dress and hair that provide adolescents with a way of playing out alternatives to traditional Hindu ways. The primary question that she addresses is, How do these young people cope with the difficulties posed by competing sets of practices? In a move that is common in research on practices, she links this question to individual variation. She finds that most Indian adolescents resolve the conflict in dress practices—at least temporarily—by adopting the same clothing styles as their mainstream peers. Although this might suggest that the younger generation has abandoned traditional Hindu dress, Miller's description of the range of actual practices in the wider community reveals a more complex situation.

Not only is there intragroup variation in dress practices among adolescents, but even at more "assimilated" temples female adults continue to wear traditional garb. This raises the question of what will happen when the girls who are now wearing shorts to temple move into adult roles in the community. Will they continue to follow the U.S. practices of their youth or will they adopt the more conservative dress of their mothers' generation? By attending to both commonalities and patterns of variation within the group, Miller's analysis suggests that community practices provide female adolescents with a basis for continuity *and* change as they make the transition to adulthood.

Miller also finds individual differences in "blended" practices, such as wearing a gold nose stud along with jeans and a pullover. This type of practice underscores the point that conflicting practices do not necessarily constrain participants to one choice over another but can afford opportunities for creative appropriation, recombination, and integration. Such examples also invite the question of which resources in families, schools, and communities support the creation of blended or bridging practices.

Research by Margarita Azmitia, Catherine Cooper, and their colleagues on the role of mentors speaks directly to this issue. In one line of work on academic outreach programs for poor and minority students in high school and college, they found that adult and peer mentors provided both emotional and instrumental support in bridging the worlds of home/community and school (Cooper, Jackson, and Azmitia, in press). Close relationships with parents, siblings, and friends also provided key links from family to school. In another study, they found that older siblings helped younger siblings with homework in Mexican-American families in which parents had elementary educations and limited proficiency in English (Azmitia, Cooper, Garcia, and Dunbar, in press).

Mentoring comes up in quite a different way in this chapter. The issue here is that of ethnographer as mentor. Miller found herself in the enviable position of being valued as a culture broker by both adolescents and their parents. To the parents, she was a positive role model for Hindu values; to the adolescents, she was someone who was critical of her own Euro-American culture, appreciated Indian culture, and understood the dilemmas of growing up in the United States. Although valuing her for different reasons, both generations viewed her as someone who had successfully bridged the two cultures.

By providing a detailed description of the researcher's role, Miller's study exemplifies the reflexiveness that many see as a hallmark of practice perspectives (Miller, in press; Packer, 1987). The social-scientific study of children is itself a cultural practice, embedded in other practices and deserving of scrutiny in its own right (Kessen, 1983). One important implication of this perspective is that researchers are always socially positioned vis-à-vis the persons they study, even when they try to be objective experimenters or invisible observers.

Acknowledging this fact is necessary in drawing meaningful interpretations of findings. For example, one can easily imagine that adolescent girls might not report to certain interviewers that they have secret boyfriends. Knowing that the girls Miller studied saw her as a person with whom they could talk freely about such matters allows the reader to place her findings in proper methodological context so that their trustworthiness and cultural validity can be assessed.

References

Azmitia, M., Cooper, C. R., Garcia, E. E., and Dunbar, N. "The Ecology of Family Guidance in Low Income Mexican-American and European-American Families." *Social Development,* in press.

Burton, L. M., Obeidallah, D., and Allison, K. "Ethnographic Perspectives on Social Context and Adolescent Development Among Inner-City African-American Teens." In R. Jessor, A. Colby, and R. A. Shweder (eds.), *Ethnography and Human Development: Context and Meaning in Social Inquiry.* Chicago: University of Chicago Press, in press.

Cooper, C. R., Jackson, J. F., and Azmitia, M. "Multiple Selves, Multiple Worlds: Ethnically Sensitive Research with Minority Youth on Identity, Relationships, and Opportunity Structures." In V. McLoyd and L. Steinberg (eds.), *Research on Minority Adolescents' Conceptual, Methodological, and Theoretical Issues.* Hillsdale, N.J.: Erlbaum, in press.

Erikson, E. H. *Identity: Youth in Crisis.* New York: W. W. Norton, 1968.

Foucault, M. *Power-Knowledge.* London: Harvester Wheatsheaf, 1980.

Goodnow, J. J., and Warton, P. M. "Contexts and Cognitions: Taking a Pluralist View." In P. Light and G. Butterworth (eds.), *Context and Cognition.* London: Harvester Wheatsheaf, 1992.

Kessen, W. "The Child and Other Cultural Inventions." In F. Kessel and A. Siegel (eds.), *The Child and Other Cultural Inventions.* New York: Praeger, 1983.

Miller, P. J. "Instantiating Culture Through Discourse Practices: Some Personal Reflections on Socialization and How to Study It." In R. Jessor, A. Colby, and R. A. Shweder (eds.), *Ethnography and Human Development: Context and Meaning in Social Inquiry.* Chicago: University of Chicago Press, in press.

Ogbu, J. U. "Cultural Mode, Identity, and Literacy." In J. W. Stigler, R. A. Shweder, and G. Herdt (eds.), *Cultural Psychology: Essays on Comparative Human Development.* New York: Cambridge University Press, 1990.

Packer, M. J. "Social Interaction as Practical Activity: Implications for the Study of Social and Moral Development." In W. Kurtines and J. Gewirtz (eds.), *Moral Development Through Social Interaction.* New York: Wiley, 1987.

Phelan, P., Davidson, A. L., and Caro, H. T. "Students' Multiple Worlds: Navigating the Borders of Family, Peer, and School Cultures." In P. Phelan and A. L. Davidson (eds.), *Cultural Diversity: Implications for Education.* New York: Teachers College Press, in press.

Quinn, N., and Holland, D. "Culture and Cognition." In D. Holland and N. Quinn (eds.), *Cultural Models in Language and Thought.* New York: Cambridge University Press, 1987.

The case of Indian Hindu adolescent youths in the United States reveals a range of variation in patterns of belief and behavior related to identity formation. Multidisciplinary and participatory methods for studying precepts and practices help expose social variation.

Precepts and Practices: Researching Identity Formation Among Indian Hindu Adolescents in the United States

Barbara D. Miller

The basic question this chapter considers is how children of immigrant communities deal with the cultural constraints and opportunities offered to them as members of both their "culture of origin" and their "culture of destination" as they make choices about identity formation. The specific case of Indian Hindu adolescent youths in the United States reveals the range of variation in adaptation patterns in belief and behavior.

I use anthropological/sociological participatory methods in my study of adolescent precepts and practices. Throughout the research, which is still in progress in 1994, I have sought to include the adolescents themselves as much as possible in shaping the study. For example, youths at a summer camp helped me design a simple questionnaire discussed in the later section on practice. Later that year, I told participants at a youth meeting about the preliminary results of the data analysis and tried to engage them in discussion of these findings.

This aspect of the research approach exemplifies what Giddens (Cassell, 1993, pp. 152–153) terms the "double hermeneutic." That term encapsulates the intertwining of the researcher's questions and presence with the ongoing construction of the cultural system of the participants in the study. In Giddens's words, the adolescents' "first-order" concepts are what I study and are the source from which I generate analytical "second-order" concepts; in sharing my findings with the adolescents, my "second-order" concepts may then become their "first-order" concepts. Thus, in engaged/participatory research, fluidity between the researcher and the researched exists and is recognized as an unavoidable and real part of the process, not as something that must be avoided or denied for the sake of some unobtainable form of "pure" research.

This chapter begins with general comments on the economic, political, and demographic features of the Indian Hindu community in the United States. I then discuss aspects of method. The rest of the chapter describes preliminary findings on precepts and practices related to identity formation among Indian Hindu youth in the United States. I pay special attention to practices related to dress and hair behaviors and highlight gender differences in bicultural adaptations. The final section presents a set of questions for further research that are prompted by this preliminary study.

Structural Features of the Study Population

The children discussed in this chapter were born to parents who emigrated to the United States after the 1967 change in the immigration law, which opened immigration to professionals and other highly educated people (Madhavan, 1985). This large influx of relatively well-off migrants was followed by subsequent migration flows from India characterized by lower education and income levels.

Structural (economic, political, and demographic) factors that affect how children will form their identities include the economic status of the family in their situations of origin and of destination (Did the family experience major changes in economic status because of their relocation?), the political status of the community within the receiving society (Is the immigrant community subject to public stigma?), and demographic features (How does density of the Indian population affect their adaptive strategies?). While structural factors are a key part of the overall social and symbolic system within which Indian Hindu adolescents in this country make choices and act, this chapter focuses more on the actual practices and related precepts of the actors themselves, taking practices as the pivotal point for research on the production and reproduction of the social system (Giddens, 1990).

The families of the adolescents being discussed here are typically well-off. In many families, both parents work and both are professionals drawing good salaries. Many of the adolescents attend or have attended expensive private high schools and universities. There are exceptions, of course: families that are struggling to make ends meet, a family in which the parents—their business having failed—returned to India leaving a college-age child behind to attend on his own. In areas outside this study—especially New Jersey, where the density of working-class Indians is high—income levels are low and declining in the early 1990s.

Politically, the adult Indian Hindu community in the United States tends to favor a low profile, with few members serving in public office, and the predominant party affiliation is Republican. Relationships between Indian immigrant groups and the larger, mainstream U.S. society vary, depending on the community of residence. Discrimination against Indian immigrant groups can be severe, ranging from the "dot-buster" violence in New Jersey (perpetrated by white racist "skinheads") to subtle forms of job discrimination that are difficult to document statistically. Grade school Indian-descent children sometimes tell me painful stories of teasing and mockery experienced in school, though more positive experiences are also reported (including reduction of such racist teasing after a "special event" on India held in the classroom). Older adolescents report that racist comments and discrimination decrease in high school and are nonexistent in college.

Demographically, most of the Indian-descent children born to parents in this wave of immigrants are now in their teens and young twenties; their parents are in their forties. Many of the offspring are old enough to be getting married, and that phase of the life cycle will prove important to watch: many U.S.-raised Indian-descent adolescents appear to be opting to retain the arranged marriage system.

The demographic distinctiveness of the Indian immigrant population in the United States—its age distribution and its predominantly high income and education levels—is producing what could be called an Indian adolescent boom in U.S. colleges and universities. Increased enrollments of Indian-Americans in courses on Indian culture is another notable recent change, and one that will pass as the boom cohort moves along.

Families of these first-generation youths live mainly in large urban centers in New York, New Jersey, Texas, and California (Helweg and Helweg, 1990; Gibson, 1988; Gardner, Robey, and Smith, 1985; Dasgupta, 1989). Many, however, are more isolated; for example, one family is headed by a physician who took a position in a small West Virginia town, and another owns a motel in a rural area in the Deep South like that depicted in the film *Mississippi Masala*. Location and, by implication, density and wealth of the Indian immigrant community affect the degree of exposure of Hindu adolescents to Indian Hindu culture.

Hinduism and Youth Culture in the United States

In larger cities with more Indian immigrant families, one increasingly finds Hindu temples and "ethnic" associations (such as special groups of Gujaratis, Bengalis, or Punjabis). Two periodicals are especially widely read in such areas: *India Abroad*, which along with news offers information on activities and events related to ethnically specialized organizations, and *Hinduism Today*, which contains articles on such matters as proper dress in Hindu temples, the value of vegetarianism, and "marriage is forever."

Pittsburgh is a major center of Hindu cultural strength; youths there are actively involved in learning about their religious and cultural heritage. The first major Hindu temple in the United States, the Sri Venkateswara Temple in Penn Hills (a suburb of Pittsburgh), is an internationally known pilgrimage site for Hindus. In Murrysville, another suburb of Pittsburgh, is a smaller temple formed after a split from the Sri Venkateswara temple: the Hindu-Jain

Temple that houses both Jain and Hindu deities and celebrates rituals in each tradition.

In many cities, Sunday schools for children are held in temples or in neighborhood centers. Nationwide, annual summer camps at which children are further enculturated into "Hindu values" and participate in secular activities such as hiking and swimming are increasingly popular.

The temples often sponsor cultural events, such as concerts and dance performances. They may provide extracurricular classes in Sanskrit and other Indian languages and lessons in music (vocal, instrumental), dance, and yoga.

Major temples, since the first one was built in Pittsburgh, have proliferated in the United States. Washington, D.C., Chicago, Austin, Boston, and many other cities now have large and impressive temples that serve local Hindus and attract many pilgrims from the United States and abroad.

Priests have been brought from India to serve in temples in the United States, and they are an important part of the socialization process for children. They attend summer camps, give talks on values, and teach children Hindu hymns. Many parents, though they are laypersons, have devoted much time to learning about Hinduism so that they can be Sunday school teachers. They comment that they, as children, learned about Hinduism "naturally," in an everyday way, but now are having to learn it more formally in order to pass it on to their children. Many parents have also taken on the role of teaching languages to children as part of Sunday school.

One obvious function of all of these temple constructions and activities vis-à-vis children is retention of Hindu values and instruction in the scriptures and key teachings, such as *ahimsa* (nonviolence), vegetarianism, and self-control.

Research Approaches

Since 1990, I have been conducting sporadic fieldwork with Hindu and Jain communities in several locations in the eastern United States. As a participant-observer in many temple, school, and summer camp activities, I serve as a speaker (sometimes invited to talk about my other research on women's status in India or my appreciation of Hindu values and teachings), as a friend, and sometimes, more formally, as a sponsor of a university South Asia student club. I try always to explain that I am also interested in learning about Hindu youth culture and that I may try to write a book about it in the future. I am often seen taking notes during youth club meetings or at a summer camp.

I have done participant-observation at several Hindu temples (including regular and irregular ritual occasions and monthly youth meetings), at summer camps for children and teenagers, at special youth events (such as temple overnights), and at special events organized by East Coast college students (including the first conference of the National Hindu Students Council, held in Pittsburgh, and the fifth South Asia Society meeting in Washington, D.C.). I have also conducted informal interviews, in person and over the telephone, with several youths. Besides talking with and observing adolescents in their everyday life (in college classrooms, in temples, at special "cultural" events), I have talked with many parents in their homes and in public areas such as temples.

In order to maintain complete anonymity for all these people, I blur in this presentation the places in which I have gathered data. I also avoid any kind of personal specificity that might reveal the identity of an individual. (Despite the anonymity, however, my gratitude to everyone who has spent time helping me learn about Hindu youth culture in the United States is deep and sincere.)

Another tricky ethical matter is the fuzzy line between formal research (when people know that I am observing them and conversing with them for research purposes) and the informal learning that often happens in the domain of "public culture"—at a shopping mall or amusement park, for instance. I assume that, in the latter instance, it is acceptable to incorporate relevant material if I treat it respectfully.

The parents of the precollege youths, the age group with whom I have spent most of my research time, tend to view me as a kind of role model for "Hindu values," even though I am a white Euro-American and was not raised as a Hindu. There are several reasons for this: I appreciate much about Hinduism, I sometimes wear Indian clothes when I attend the temple or special events, I can speak some Hindi, I am somewhat vegetarian, I have spent long periods of time in India, I am a professor, and I appear to know and appreciate quite a bit about Indian culture. Sometimes being a Euro-American is a surprising plus: since Hindus in the United States are used to interacting with Americans who know little more about India than the usual stereotypes of poverty and population problems, many parents—those who see me as a role model of someone who appreciates Hindu culture and values and has learned much about it—value my interactions with their children.

The precollege children and youths see me as someone who is interesting and entertaining: I offer them the view of someone who is critical of her own culture in some respects and has positive feelings about Indian culture. Even though my age puts me in the "parent" generation, because I am "American" many of the adolescents see me as being able to share with them their feelings about the problems of growing up in the United States (problems related to dating, sexuality) and as being more liberal than many of their parents. This is not so true of the elementary school children, most of whom are not yet facing some of the identity issues that their older siblings are.

So, while many of the parents see me as representing "traditional" values, many of the children see me as representing more liberal values. But both groups, I believe, also view me as a person who has been able to bridge—at least partially—two cultural traditions, the American/Western and the Indian/Eastern.

My fieldwork is ongoing and preliminary. At this stage, I have more breadth than depth. I have much information on precepts and practices among cross sections of diverse groups of youths. In contrast, I have only spotty detailed information gathered from private interviews on more sensitive topics (body image, sexuality, guilt, attitudes about God, and so on). In other words, I have more information on "public" precepts and practices—those that I have observed and have studied through questionnaires—than on "private" or "secret" ones (Eicher, Baizerman, and Michelman, 1991).

Variations in Precepts

The youths whom I have met and talked with range from quiet, studious paragons of "Hindu values" as espoused by the more conservative parents (these are usually the younger kids) to outspoken campus radicals who sneer at the bourgeois values of their double-doctor parental configurations. I have heard a college student present a carefully prepared enunciation of the value of premarital chastity, and I have heard other students make comments such as, "Nobody really takes chastity seriously anymore."

This is not, in other words, a population evidencing a high degree of consensus on some very important issues. On the other hand, these young people all face some similar questions as children of immigrant Indian Hindus, and these questions are deep and potentially troubling ones. They concern problems of identity (which all children and adolescents face, but immigrant children more so) and problems of meaning, and they concern the multiple and often conflicting scripts about their potential identity that are being handed to them by parents, grandparents, schools, temples, friends, the media, summer camp, conferences, an anthropologist/friend/adviser.

In their daily lives, they are presented with "precepts" from both their Hindu heritage and from "mainstream" U.S. culture: on one hand, they have their parents and various aspects of Hindu cultural exposure, including temple activities, summer camps, the Indian Students Association at college, and various Indian cultural publications; on the other hand, they have Euro-American and other non-Indian school peers, school teachers, and media options.

Some features of Hinduism receive special emphasis because of the immigrant context. High parental anxiety about dating and premarital sex no doubt drives the emphasis I have seen in more conservative families on gender segregation that is more or less explicit. Many high school age girls and boys are not allowed to date at all, though many do so surreptitiously. A major flap occurred at one summer camp because an adult counselor did not want boys and girls to sit together in gender-mixed groups during discussion sessions.

Debates and discussions at temples and in homes about dating are often heated. Dating, and the unspoken fear among many parents of premarital sexual relationships, pervades conversations between many parents. As Indian psychoanalyst Sudhir Kakar (1986, p. 39) notes, "In sexual terms, the West is perceived as a gigantic brothel, whereas the 'good' Indian woman is idealized nostalgically in all her purity, modesty and chastity. For Indians living in the West, this idealization and the splitting that underlies it are more emotionally charged and more intense than would be the case in India itself. The inevitable Westernization of wives and daughters is, therefore, the cause of deep emotional stress in men, and of explosive conflicts in the family." These conflicts may cause emotional stress in the wives and daughters too.

Another topic that is heatedly discussed among teenagers is the rule that menstruating women should not go to the temple. Many of the adolescents, raised in a culture that states the value of gender equality, see this as an unfair restriction. This is another classic example of the apparent conflict between gender-egalitarian teachings in U.S. schools (in spite of the fact that gender equality is not achieved in U.S. schools or public life) and the gender-inegalitarian rules of certain aspects of Hinduism.

Variations in Practices

"Practices" are taken here to be people's routine activities, which are inextricably linked both to the structures within which actors operate and to the meaning that actors give to their activities. In themselves, practices contain both structure and meaning in some sense, and they are the basis for transformation and change in structure and meaning. Practices are the everyday pivot between structure and the individual.

My understanding to date of adolescent Hindu practices is limited to some participant-observation of everyday life and questionnaire data that reveal preference hierarchies about certain practices. An important next step would be to pursue other methods, including time allocation studies, a diary approach, in-depth interviews, and yearly follow-up questionnaires about Hinduism-related practices at several summer camps.

The questionnaire I have used thus far was developed on the spur of the moment at a Hindu summer camp for children from fourth grade through high school. As I noted earlier, the youths at the camp, especially the older, precollege students, offered suggestions for the categories included in the questionnaire.

The questionnaire is necessarily simple: I hand-wrote the final copy sitting at a picnic table, and photocopies were made in a nearby small town. I generated a beginning list of potentially important "Hindu values" based on my general knowledge of Hinduism and what the youths were being taught at Sunday school and camp. The students then suggested additional categories, and so did one or two adult counselors. Everyone seemed positive about the questionnaire, and one head counselor hoped that the questionnaire data would be useful in showing that the camp actually promotes Hindu values in children who repeatedly attend. The youths themselves were also interested in learning about the results.

A total of eighty-seven youths answered the questionnaire, including forty boys and forty-seven girls. The age distribution was roughly equal for most ages, ranging from the smallest cohort of seven nine-year-olds to the largest of twenty-one thirteen-year-olds. Only five respondents were aged fifteen years and older; most of them were volunteer youth counselors.

The Hindu values listed on the questionnaire range from key teachings of Hinduism about the importance of *satya,* or truthfulness (I generally use the English terms, unless there is no obvious equivalent, as for *pranayama,* breathing exercises, or unless the Hindu term is one everyone knows and uses, as for *yoga),* to "saying grace before meals," which is not, to my knowledge, a Hindu practice at all, but which several adolescents urged me to put on the questionnaire. Hinduism, especially as it is learned in the United States, is a religion of acts, of practices. One highly respected path to being a Hindu is through one's acts, *karma yoga,* the path of deeds. During a discussion session with precollege adolescents at one summer camp, the question was raised as to whether I could be a Hindu even though I had not been born one. The temple priest, who was sitting with our group, was asked to comment, and he said that indeed I was a Hindu through my acts, at which point a round of approving applause broke out.

Although this questionnaire does not provide any data on what Hindu youths actually do, it does get one step closer to understanding their practices by asking them to comment on what they think are important practices relating to being a Hindu. Some patterns have emerged from my preliminary, noncomputerized analysis of the questionnaire responses.

Resoundingly, across both genders and all age groups, the following three values were judged to be most important: truthfulness, self-control, and respect for others. Only one twelve-year-old male and one fifteen-year-old female said that being truthful was not important to being a good Hindu, and the same two respondents said that self-control was not important. Only one eleven-year-old male said that respect for others was not important.

"Belief in God" and "daily prayer" were nearly as highly ranked as the top three, but they received more "average" rankings than "high." "Reading the Hindu scriptures" and "singing *bhajans*" (sacred hymns) followed in importance, along with attending Sunday school. Over the age groups, there was a tendency for the older children to rank these last aspects of Hindu practices lower than did the elementary school children.

The categories that received the lowest rankings in importance were fasting, *pranayama* (breathing exercises), and listening to Indian music. Fifty-two respondents thought listening to Indian music was not important, while eight thought it was very important. Forty-seven respondents thought fasting was not important, while seven thought it was very important (four younger males and three older females). Thirty-two respondents thought *pranayama* was not important, while thirteen thought it very important (again younger males and older females). Other practices that followed closely in degrees of unimportance were meditation, wearing Indian clothing, attending Sunday school, talking with friends about Hinduism, and being vegetarian.

These factors are a mix of more "secular" practices, such as listening to Indian music, and more "religious" practices, such as meditation (which is a key Hindu teaching). Further research would reveal whether or not listening to Indian music was given a low rating because respondents perceived it not to relate directly to Hindu religious values or because they did not like to listen to it. Likewise, further research could address why meditation was ranked so much lower than yoga, which received strong "average" marks. Perhaps it was because yoga is more acceptable in mainstream U.S. society, which emphasizes and values physical exercise and which recognizes the "scientific" value of yogalike practices. Additionally, summer camps often involve morning yoga classes, so the students know about it and can do it.

Dress as Practice

Dress practices are receiving increasing research attention, and this impetus seems especially warranted for adolescent age groups, since adolescents, by definition in middle-class and upper-class U.S. society, are searching for ways to shape and express their identity (Littrell, Damhorst, and Littrell, 1990). "Looks" is an important part of this process. The individual pursuit of "looks" is spurred on by structural features of this country's beauty economy that promote beauty and hair practices that cost money to achieve and maintain (Lakoff and Scherr, 1984; Haug, 1986; Freedman, 1986; Ewen, 1990). In addition, people who "look" right are at an advantage when it comes to achieving such desired ends as dates, school success, and jobs (Driskell, 1983; Heilman and Stopeck, 1985).

Mainstream U.S. dress styles and Hindu modesty codes clash most directly and resoundingly for girls. "Traditional" Hindu standards of female modesty that mandate that most of the body be covered (especially legs) in the public domain are being challenged in the United States. For boys, the more or less universal dress style of the West (with the exception of shorts) works for both cultural traditions.

Discussions about appropriate dress at the temple outline the conflicts most clearly. Given my experience in India with female modesty codes, I was shocked when I first saw high school–age girls wearing shorts at a temple event in this country. While adult women at the temple are generally quite modestly dressed, usually in a *sari* or *kurta/pajama* outfit, the dress of female youths varies considerably, depending on the season and the event. At the Hindu-Jain Temple in Murrysville, young girls wear Indian-style clothing only at very special events, such as a sacred thread ceremony: for those special occasions, girls don *punjabi* suits (*selwar/kameez, kurta/pajama*), while boys, like the men, wear Western shirts and pants or even shorts in the summer. Some temples are now considering adopting a dress code.

Dress can be a sign of degree of assimilation into mainstream U.S. culture. Given the pressures on adolescents to conform to this or that look (clothes from the Gap one year, clothes from Eddie Bauer the next), most youths in public places such as malls and sports events are dressed nearly identically. At Pittsburgh's Hindu-Jain temple, at regular temple worship events (such as first Sundays in the month, when there is a *havan*, or sacred fire), members of the youth group are notably unmarked by any Indian clothing or ornaments. At monthly youth group meetings, I saw only one Indian cultural marker: a female leader of the youth group began wearing a tiny gold nose stud, though the rest of her clothing and accessories looked like a typical Gap outfit: pullover and jeans.

In contrast, adolescent females at a dominantly South Indian temple in Pittsburgh (which is, many Indians say, less "acculturated" than the more North Indian temple) more often wear *punjabis* and *bindis* (forehead dots). I have never seen a *bindi* on other than adult women at the Hindu-Jain temple.

At a South Asia Society conference in the early 1990s, which drew several hundred college students mainly from eastern universities to a three-day meeting at George Washington University and Georgetown University in Washington, D.C., only a few students wore overtly "South Asian" clothing: one Sikh male wearing a turban, one Bangladeshi female with her hair covered by a scarf, and two older females in *punjabis*. There were no *bindis*, no nose studs, no *saris*.

Hair Practices

In India, rules for female hair care are longstanding and play prominent roles in classic myths and epics. In a well-known part of the epic *Mahabharata,* for example, the heroine Draupadi refuses to wash and braid her hair until she has had vengeance on an enemy. The general ideal, again defined for females but not for males, is that hair should never be cut and should be black (not grayed by age or discolored by malnutrition). Young girls generally wear their hair in a double or single braid, while married women keep hair tied in a bun or single braid. Unbound hair for a woman signals that she is menstruating, is in mourning, or is in some other special state (Hiltebeitel, 1991).

In contemporary India, girls and women in urban centers are increasingly seen with unbound, cropped, or Western-styled loose hair. The same applies, in general, to Hindu adolescent girls in the United States. Here one rarely sees the traditional single braid on a college-age female, though ponytails and fancy colored ponytail holders are popular. Ponytails provide some continuity with more traditional hair-binding styles, though contemporary "crimps" (made of fluffy chiffon or silk) tend to allow looseness rather than provide strict control of hair.

Age is an important factor affecting Hindu females' hair practices. My observations at two summer camps reveal that many of the youngest girls, between eight and ten years, begin practicing beauty and hair routines every day. A telltale sign is the omnipresent "kaboodle," a plastic box with an upper and lower level and a mirror in the lid. (See the informative discussion of mirrors in Freedman, 1986, pp. 23–25, 33–37.) The kaboodle contains makeup, combs and brushes, hair clips and pins, and even a blow-dryer. Kaboodles are opened and fiddled with by some girls in this age group several times a day. At camp, frequent interactions between the girls center around playing with and fixing one another's hair.

Most little girls that I know in this young age group have hair that is at least shoulder length, but one notable exception is a very perky and funny little girl whose hair is chin length. Another case is remarkable because both she and her mother have chin-length hair, and the mother is among the more outspoken and active of the women. In fact, mother-daughter hair parallels are quite common.

Fathers, it appears, have more conservative attitudes about hair length, and many girls have told me that it is their fathers who most object to their cutting their hair. I once complimented a little girl on her long hair and asked her if she liked it better than short hair. She said yes but that her father hated short hair. (In the future, I intend to interview some fathers on the topic of daughters' hair length.)

In the high school–age category, one begins to see hair that is more obviously managed—hair in the lioness/sexy category, hair with a side part instead of the traditional center part, hair that changes its style in the course of a day. I know one girl with very long, loose hair and bangs that drape over an eye who has to hold her hair with one hand when she eats so that she can get food into her mouth. Single or double braids are not a common style of high school girls, but a high "clinch" or ponytail or loose bun with a cloth crimp can do the trick of attractive but relaxed containment. Tightly pulled hair is not seen.

Chin-length hair is more common on older girls than among the younger set, and even the occasional pixie-style cut can be seen. One girl of precollege age had a dramatically short and stylish haircut; she was also one of the most consistently outspoken members of her youth group. In her case, the short hair may have been a sign of rebellion against her father, who was very strict, but I have no data that could shed light on this possibility.

So far, I have seen only two high school girls who obviously lightened the color of their hair, and they both sat together at the meeting we attended. Perms are not much in evidence, although I have heard that parent-child conflicts sometimes erupt because the daughter wants a perm and the parents say no.

At summer camp, no high school girl would appear at the first morning event (prayers) with wet hair, although some of the younger ones would. It is a matter of quiet amusement among the adults at camp how early the high school girls will get up in order to shower, shampoo their hair, style their hair, and apply makeup. One summer, a new rule was promulgated by the adult camp committee: in each of the girls' cabins, no more than three blow-dryers could be used at one time, because there had been several electrical outages due to circuit overloads.

Unfortunately, I know less about grooming among the boys. While there are variations in hair cut—from brush cuts to longer, more drapey looks—the essential look to me is more uniform than among the girls. I do know, however, as the mother of a teenage son, that achieving what seems to me a "non-look" can take a lot of time and psychic energy every morning.

Future Questions About Gender Differences in Bicultural Identity Formation

This preliminary research prompts more questions than it answers, especially in the area of possible differences in the responses of Indian Hindu girls and boys in identity formation in the United States. Bicultural pressures on Hindu girls appear to be stronger than on boys and may affect their development in several ways.

Identity formation and sexuality. Dual pressures on Indian-descent girls come from the direction of mainstream U.S. culture to be popular and date and from their parents not to be popular and not to date—in other words, to look like a Barbie doll but remain a virgin until marriage. How do girls vary in their handling of pressures about female modesty and chastity? How do parents differ in their evaluations of female behavior, and how do parents' evaluations affect a daughter's sexual identity formation?

Identity formation and cultural guilt. Many young girls of Hindu descent in the United States experience serious levels of guilt as they try both to please their parents by meeting requirements about no dates and no boyfriends and definitely no premarital sex and to be part of the peer culture of high school and college. Several high school and college females have told me about the lies they tell their parents so that they can get some extra time at night to be out with their boyfriend. Some have a secret boyfriend that they feel they cannot tell their parents about because of the likelihood of being forbidden to see him or go out at all. How do boys and girls differ in terms of their internalization of guilt (or some South Asian variation on the theme of self-blame and remorse)? How serious do such feelings become, and how do the children deal with them (talking with friends, parents, teachers, and so on)?

Identity formation and social networks. Cultural anthropologist Gananath Obeyesekere offers the concept of "estrangement" to refer to an individual's being cut off from his or her own self, culture, and society (1981, p. 104). It causes "illness" through inhibiting the performance of normal social roles. Aparna Rayaprol's research on women's participation in the Sri Venkateswara temple in Pittsburgh similarly demonstrates the importance of the temple in the reconstruction of social networks and personal identity among these women (1994). For adolescent Hindu girls in the United States, religious options for dealing with possible estrangement are less clear than for adult women, given the pressures on them to conform to mainstream U.S. society in school and the pressures at home not to conform. How do different patterns of participation in temple groups and activities affect girls' and boys' feelings of self-worth and well-being? What happens to children who live in areas where no temple exists to provide social support networks?

Identity formation and autonomy. Going away to college offers young people increased autonomy of decision making. Unless the college student continues to live at home, the student will no longer have to lie about where she is going at night if it happens to be a date with a boyfriend, nor will she have to be home at a particular hour. But this freedom may not be stress-free. Brumberg's writing (1988) on adolescence suggests that it is possible that the combined pressures of the morality infusion received from parents, peer pressure at college, and the pressure to be "autonomous" may lead to problems among these young women, typically eating disorders. Other body-related afflictions are also possible, such as negative body image and low self-esteem. The traditional Indian value of controlled food intake by girls and women may cross over into the American dieting/thinness/perfectionism/parental-overcontrol syndrome, perhaps placing girls of Indian descent at unusually high risk of eating disorders and other body-related disorders (Khandelwal and Saxena, 1990; see also the cross-cultural presentation in Fabrega and Miller, in press). What is the distribution of recognizable disorders in Indian-descent girls as compared to girls of other ethnic groups, and what are the possible effects of bicultural strains?

Identity formation and educational achievement. My observations indicate that the path to success for Indian boys in the United States is easier than for girls. It is more integrated, because brains and efficacy achieve success on all fronts—with parents, in school or college, and with the opposite sex. Another potential source of stress that affects adolescent Hindu girls more than boys may come from unconscious parental derailment of a daughter's wish to pursue certain careers or even to go away for college (Holland and Eisenhart, 1990). Indian Hindu daughters tend to have to fight harder to get to go away for college than their brothers, who are allowed greater spatial autonomy. (This pattern is observable among many Euro-American families too.) Such subtle steering or outright differential tracking can result in several outcomes—actual rebellion, feelings of low self-worth, and resentment. In one case, parental refusal to allow a daughter to attend the college of her choice seemed directly related to her intense desire to get away from her parents at any cost. Ultimately, her desire for escape led her to consent to an arranged marriage to a boy she had never met in a different U.S. city. What are the patterns of gender-differential socialization concerning educational goals and career attainment? Do they differ for girls who are only children as compared to girls from larger sibling sets? How do girls (compared to boys) resist or accommodate to their parents' wishes and guidance about their careers?

Identity formation and support systems. While cultural pressures from such Hindu institutions as temples and summer camps may create greater strains for Hindu girls than boys, it is simultaneously possible that the peer-group bonding offered by such groups helps support these girls during adolescent identity formation. Thus girls whose parents pressure them but who live in isolated areas where there are no youth groups may be at the highest risk of bicultural strain. This issue warrants further study as well.

Hindu Youths in the United States in Perspective

The Indian-descent Hindu youth population of the United States, as of the early 1990s, is an unusual immigrant group in many ways. They are generally of well-off parents, highly educated, and highly motivated to achieve.

Bicultural strains emerge between certain Hindu values that conflict with some mainstream U.S. norms and practices. Youths, especially girls, may be caught between these two cultural systems and feel strain in trying to accommodate to both.

The patterns of choice and accommodation made by Hindu youths in this country are culturally specific to that group at this time. One would expect different findings for Chinese-Americans, Mexican-Americans, or immigrant groups who experience downward rather than upward social mobility in their move. Given the pervasive presence of new and old immigrant communities in the United States, it is increasingly important that researchers pay attention to the strategies and potential strains faced by youths as they come to terms with several (and sometimes competing) cultural options regarding their precepts and practices.

References

Brumberg, J. *Fasting Girls: The History of Anorexia Nervosa.* New York: Plume, 1988.

Cassell, P. *The Giddens Reader.* Palo Alto, Calif.: Stanford University Press, 1993.

Dasgupta, S. S. *On the Trail of an Uncertain Dream: Indian Immigrant Experience in America.* New York: AMS Press, 1989.

Driskell, E. J. "Beauty as Status." *American Journal of Sociology,* 1983, *89* (1), 140–165.

Eicher, J. B., Baizerman, S., and Michelman, J. "Adolescent Dress, Part II: A Qualitative Study of Suburban High School Students." *Adolescence,* 1991, *26* (103), 679–686.

Ewen, S. *All Consuming Images: The Politics of Style in Contemporary Culture.* New York: Basic Books, 1990.

Fabrega, H., and Miller, B. "Adolescent Psychology and Medical Anthropology." *Medical Anthropology Quarterly,* in press.

Freedman, R. *Beauty Bound.* New York: Lexington Books, 1986.

Gardner, R. W., Robey, B., and Smith, P. C. "Asian Americans: Growth, Change, and Diversity." *Population Bulletin,* 1985, *40* (4), 3–43.

Gibson, Margaret A. *Accommodation Without Assimilation: Sikh Immigrants in an American High School.* Ithaca, N.Y.: Cornell University Press, 1988.

Giddens, A. *Central Problems in Social Theory: Action, Structure, and Contradiction in Social Analysis.* Berkeley: University of California Press, 1990.

Haug, W. F. *Critique of Commodity Aesthetics: Appearance, Sexuality, and Advertising in Capitalist Society.* (R. Bock, trans.) Minneapolis: University of Minnesota Press, 1986.

Heilman, M. I., and Stopeck, M. H. "Attractiveness and Corporate Success: Different Causal Attributions for Males and Females." *Journal of Applied Psychology,* 1985, *70,* 379–388.

Helweg, A., and Helweg, U. *An Immigrant Success Story: East Indians in America.* Philadelphia: University of Pennsylvania Press, 1990.

Hiltebeitel, A. *The Cult of Draupadi 2: On Hindu Ritual and the Goddess.* Chicago: University of Chicago Press, 1991.

Holland, D. C., and Eisenhart, M. A. *Educated in Romance: Women, Achievement, and College Culture.* Chicago: University of Chicago Press, 1990.

Kakar, S. "Male and Female in India: Identity Formation and Its Effects on Cultural Adaptation in Tradition and Transformation." In R. H. Brown and G. V. Coelho (eds.), *Asian Indians in America.* Williamsburg, Va.: College of William and Mary, 1986.

Khandelwal, S. K., and Saxena, S. "Anorexia Nervosa in Adolescents of Asian Extraction." *British Journal of Psychiatry,* 1990, *157,* 784.

Lakoff, R. T., and Scherr, R. L. *Face Value: The Politics of Beauty.* New York: Routledge & Kegan Paul, 1984.

Littrell, M. A., Damhorst, M. L., and Littrell, J. M. "Clothing Interests, Body Satisfaction, and Eating Behavior of Adolescent Females: Related or Independent Dimensions?" *Adolescence,* 1990, 25 (97), 77–95.

Madhavan, M. C., "Indian Emigrants: Numbers, Characteristics, and Economic Impact." *Population and Development Review,* 1985, 11 (3), 457–481.

Obeyesekere, G. *Medusa's Hair: An Essay on Personal Symbols and Religious Experience.* Chicago: University of Chicago Press, 1981.

Rayaprol, A. "Gender in the Making of an Immigrant Community: A Study of South Indian Immigrants in Pittsburgh." Unpublished doctoral dissertation, Department of Sociology, University of Pittsburgh, 1994.

Saran, P. *The Asian Indian Experience in the United States.* Cambridge, Mass.: Schenkman, 1985.

BARBARA D. MILLER is associate professor of anthropology and international affairs and director, Women's Studies Program, George Washington University, Washington, D.C.

Editors' Preface to "Cultural Practices and the Conception of Individual Differences"

As we noted earlier, the purpose of these chapter prefaces is to highlight some of the issues that each chapter raises and to "place" each chapter, both in relation to the other three in the set and in relation to other research and to the general questions raised by a cultural practices perspective.

Terezinha Nunes's chapter raises especially the question, What are the consequences, both cognitive and social, of engaging in a particular practice? It is clearly not sufficient to say that "participation influences development" or that "development is in itself a change in participation." We need to ask what particular aspects of a practice have particular consequences. The aspects emphasized, and the consequences to which they are linked, may vary, but the specification is essential.

One of the consequences that has gained prominence has to do with the extent to which what is learned remains linked to the situation in which it is learned or comes to be used in other situations. That issue has been underlined by reports of what Nunes calls "intra-individual variability." To use one of her examples, sometimes people can solve a problem when they are asked to solve it "in their heads" but not when it is presented on paper. To use an example from Cole, Gay, Glick, and Sharp (1971), people can solve an arithmetic problem in everyday life but not when the "same problem" is presented as part of a Western-type measure of ability.

Such variability, as Nunes points out, is a challenge to any theory of general abilities: general abilities should give rise to performances that are much the same across situations. It is also a challenge to our usual picture of devel-

opment as a process of increasing "decontextualization" or "generalization"—
an implication emphasized by Lave (for example, Lave, 1988). We may need
to regard strategies that cut across situations as special cases rather than as the
norm. Such cases may arise, for example, only after an initial restriction to "situated" learning or only when value is placed on discovery rather than on efficient routines (Hatano and Inagaki, 1992). Alternatively, we may need to
consider thinking as always involving "tricks of the trade" that remain tied to
the problems for which we first learned them.

Using the question of variability as a springboard, Nunes offers a set of
proposals. Among these are the following:

• Cultural groups vary in the extent to which they provide experience
with particular kinds of problems and particular procedures for solving them.
Street vendors in Brazil, for instance, are not inexperienced with arithmetic
problems. The problems they are accustomed to, however, are of a particular
kind. For one thing, errors have meaning. In addition, the procedures are of a
specific kind. Most problems, for instance, are solved "orally" (by "mental
arithmetic") rather than on paper.

• The procedures learned make a difference to the kinds of error that
occur. School problems, for instance (treated as problems without meaning),
often generate meaningless answers and wild errors. Introducing meaning into
school problems may then be the way to improve performance.

• Cognitive factors may not be the only explanations for why it is that
procedures learned in some situations (in school as opposed to outside school,
for instance) are not always carried over to other situations. The procedures
used in making calculations, Nunes points out, serve both "cognitive" and
"social" functions. Using school procedures, for example, marks one's identity
as a "schooled" individual—an image one may wish either to project or to
avoid.

To establish such proposals, Nunes brings to bear a variety of ingenious
research methods. They range from the analysis of errors to experimental
changes in the way an arithmetic problem is set (changes in the task in which
a problem is embedded or in the arithmetic procedures that are suggested as
feasible). Rather than go through the several designs, we shall turn to the question, Where does this research fit with other research on practices?

We might ask that question first in terms of the links between Nunes's
chapter and the other three in the set. We chose chapters that would pick up
different aspects of practices, would demonstrate different ways to turn a conceptual question into a research strategy. There are, however, overlaps. The
chapter by Nunes picks up, for instance, a question that has appeared in all of
the discussions. Given the fact that a need can be met or a problem solved by
more than one practice, what gives rise to the emergence of one practice rather
than another? Picked up also is an interest in the way that particular practices
are linked to identity: in this case, one's sense of oneself as a person who uses
"educated" or "school-based" methods or as a person concerned with practical problems and pragmatic ways of working. The most specific overlap, how-

ever, is with the chapter by Rogoff, Baker-Sennett, Lacasa, and Goldsmith—an overlap in the form of concern with the consequences of a practice. Rogoff and her colleagues consider consequences in terms of change in the individual, in interactions between participants, and in the practice itself. Nunes keeps the focus firmly on the individual: on the ways in which arithmetic problems are perceived and solved and on the sense that particular ways of framing or solving a problem are better than others or more appropriate to the kind of person one is.

Where does the research that Nunes describes fit with still other research on practices? It is, first of all, part of a long-term program of research on both everyday and school arithmetic—research in which Nunes has often been joined by Analucia Schliemann and David Carraher. It is part also of a wide-ranging set of studies, in several cultures, of the nature and consequences of variations in number systems, number naming, and the presence of particular tools such as the abacus (for example, Ceci, 1993; Hatano, in press; Saxe, 1990; Stigler and Baranes, 1989).

From that wealth of studies, we shall single out two observations that have particular relevance to the issues we have raised about practices. The first comes from Saxe (1990). He has drawn attention to the use of parts of the body as a counting system among the Oksapmin of New Guinea and to the ways in which this system survives even when children go to school. His comments remind us that using number systems (counting on one's fingers, for instance) can clearly be as disapproved of as using sign language, using one's home language, or—to revert to Barbara Miller's example of competing systems—wearing one's hair in one style rather than another.

The other selection from these studies will dispel the sense that the particular consequences of particular arithmetic procedures call for research that takes one into exotic places with unusual approaches to calculations or mathematics. Stodolsky (1988) has placed her research on arithmetic within the classrooms of Chicago. The same teachers, she has shown, teach mathematics and social studies in different ways: the former area by "prescription" ("Let me tell you how"), the latter by "projects." Small wonder, Stodolsky points out, that most children—and most adults—come to regard mathematics problems as calling for an expert who will provide a formula but see "social" questions as allowing for some degree of individual opinion or independent research and discovery. Like the "efficiency" orientation toward looking after animals in classroom science lessons that Hatano and Inagaki (1992) find leads to less exploratory action and thinking than occurs when one raises a pet at home, lessons that involve prescriptive solutions are unlikely to encourage improvisation or lateral thinking.

The examples from Hatano and Inagaki bring us to the last point of placement. Research on the consequences of practices has by no means been limited to studies based on number practices, even though these have consistently been attractive to researchers (for example, Cole, Gay, Glick, and Sharp, 1971; Lave, 1988). Classroom practices—from the structure of question-and-answer exchanges to the way tasks are defined—have been another frequent choice (for example, Mehan, 1979; Newman, Griffin, and Cole, 1989). For a challenging contrast to the field of numbers, however, we draw attention to the practice of cooking. Here is a practice where one may use an experimental procedure such as determining how well people can proceed when asked to produce a dish without some of the standard ingredients (Hatano and Oura, 1990, cited by Hatano and Inagaki, 1992). Here is a practice where repetition can lead either to "routine expertise" or to "adaptive expertise," to reliance on the repetition of earlier steps or to freedom from prescribed ways and to improvisation (Hatano and Inagaki, 1992). What leads to one outcome rather than to another? Why, to take a further example, does repeated practice in ways of "doing gender" (West and Zimmerman, 1987) not lead to any readiness to step away from old ways? Why does it seem always to lead to the stronger and stronger conviction that particular practices are "natural" and to a lack of reflection, questioning, or ready improvisation? The several consequences of particular practices clearly present a number of questions still needing to be answered. Nunes's chapter offers a description of several ways to proceed.

References

Ceci, S. J. "Contextual Trends in Intellectual Development." *Developmental Review,* 1993, *13,* 403–435.

Cole, M., Gay, J., Glick, J., and Sharp, D. *The Cultural Context of Learning and Thinking.* New York: Basic Books, 1971.

Hatano, G. "Learning Arithmetic with an Abacus." In T. Nunes and P. Bryant (eds.), *How Do Children Learn Mathematics?* Hove, U.K.: Erlbaum, in press.

Hatano, G., and Inagaki, K. "Desituating Cognition Through the Construction of Conceptual Knowledge." In P. Light and G. Butterworth (eds.), *Context and Cognition.* London: Harvester Wheatsheaf, 1992.

Lave, J. *Cognition in Practice: Mind, Mathematics, and Culture in Everyday Life.* New York: Cambridge University Press, 1988.

Mehan, H. *Learning Lessons: Social Organization in the Classroom.* Cambridge, Mass.: Harvard University Press, 1979.

Newman, P., Griffin, P., and Cole, M. *The Construction Zone: Working for Cognitive Change in School.* New York: Cambridge University Press, 1989.

Saxe, G. B. *Culture and Cognitive Development: Studies in Mathematical Understanding.* Hillsdale, N.J.: Erlbaum, 1990.

Stigler, J. W., and Baranes, R. "Culture and Mathematics Learning." *Review of Research in Education,* 1989, *15,* 253–306.

Stodolsky, S. *The Subject Matters: Classroom Activity in Mathematics and Social Studies.* Chicago: University of Chicago Press, 1988.

West, C., and Zimmerman, D. "Doing Gender." *Gender and Society,* 1987, *1,* 125–151.

Current conceptions of individual differences locate abilities inside the person. However, empowered by their cultural tools, humans can surpass their natural abilities. This chapter considers empirical evidence and theoretical issues that point out the need to reconceptualize individual differences in psychology.

Cultural Practices and the Conception of Individual Differences: Theoretical and Empirical Considerations

Terezinha Nunes

For many years now, a certain type of evidence has been accumulating that poses a challenge to our ways of thinking in psychology. The evidence I refer to has to do with within-individual differences. The conception it challenges is a most fundamental one in psychology, because it involves some aspects of our conception of persons/individuals.

Briefly, evidence about within-individual differences has been documented in many studies where the same individuals display radically different levels of the same problem-solving ability across situations. Simple examples are adults in California who were able to solve some mathematical problems much better in the supermarket than on a mathematics test (Lave, 1988) and Brazilian children who displayed clearly superior problem-solving ability in either real or simulated shop situations over other contexts for solving mathematics problems (Carraher, Carraher, and Schliemann, 1985, 1987). The aspects of our conception of individuals that are challenged by this evidence have to do with common assertions such as these: "People have abilities" and "Some people are more or less able than others." If people *have* abilities or *are* able, why do they behave so differently across situations?

In this chapter, I want first to point out some of the contradictions I see in the current literature between the conception of individual ability and the analysis of the development of children's knowledge. The subsequent sections will discuss inputs into the development of children's knowledge that redefine our conception of individual abilities in significant ways. The arguments that follow are presented as they developed within a program of research carried out over a decade involving a large number of colleagues and students, who unfortunately cannot be properly acknowledged here. The viewpoint presented is a personal one.

The Challenge for Theories of Individual Abilities

About ten years ago, my colleagues (especially Analucia Schliemann and David Carraher) in Recife, Brazil, and I set out to study working-class children's mathematical abilities, relying very much on a textbook conception of intelligence. Irrespective of variations in other aspects, most textbooks will suggest that a child's intelligence is determined by both nature and nurture. Nature sets a basic pattern, and nurture brings it to fruition. If nature is not nurtured properly, the child's intellect cannot develop properly. These simple ideas apply both to the study of individual differences and to Piagetian conceptions of the development of logico-mathematical thinking. Both approaches to the development of intelligence lead us to expect that working-class children, who are believed to live in culturally impoverished environments, will display lower levels of logico-mathematical reasoning than their middle- and upper-class cohorts.

Clearly, issues of measurement make this picture somewhat more complex in the study of intellectual development. Motivation may influence children's performance in tasks, and we may underestimate a child's ability or level of development if evaluation is carried out under conditions that do not motivate the child properly, do not adequately convey to the child what is required in the situation, or place the child under stress. There is thus much room for the emergence of false negatives—that is, the assumption that a child lacks some reasoning ability when it does not. The possibility of false positives has always been a lesser concern in the measurement of intelligence because of the basic assumption that nurture cannot surpass nature. If tasks are constructed in such a way as to minimize correct responses for the wrong reasons (for example, by chance or based on inadequate reasoning), false positives are much too unlikely to be an issue.

Quite early in our research program, we became concerned with the issue of false negatives. Cole, Gay, Glick, and Sharp (1971), Labov (1970), Donaldson (1978), Perret-Clermont (1980), and many others had emphasized that false negatives might be much more common in the evaluation of intellectual abilities than had been thought. Further, the work of Greenfield (1966) had alerted us to the effects on intellectual development of a powerful nurturing place, school. Mindful of these forewarnings, we set out to study the development of mathematical reasoning in Recife's poor children.

In our first study (Nunes Carraher and Schliemann, 1983), we compared poor and middle-class children's performance on mathematical tasks while controlling for the mathematical instruction received. That meant that the children from these two backgrounds had different age levels as a consequence of local educational provision. As a rule, Brazilian middle- and upper-class children learn to read in preschool and then attend a private primary school. Their first-grade teachers can dedicate much more time to mathematics teaching than the teachers in state-supported schools, attended by poor children, because first-graders in state schools need the time for reading instruction. Conscious of the need to avoid false negatives, we administered the tasks individually, allowing the children to explain to us their procedures during the interviews. We found almost no differences between poor and middle-class children in their performance in problem-solving and Piagetian tasks (Nunes Carraher and Schliemann, 1983), but a larger percentage of the poor children (32 percent) than the middle-class children (2 percent) failed in school arithmetic at the end of the year. Thus the poor children's performance was unstable; whereas they were successful in our tasks, they failed in school. Was this a case of schools coming up with "false negatives"? Could it really be the case that poor children learn mathematics outside school and somehow fail to display their knowledge in school tests?

In the next two studies, we investigated this variability in their performance in greater detail. In search for a *context* in which poor children might learn mathematics outside school, we thought about the informal economy—a sector of the economy that involves street-vending and in which youngsters from poor families are often active. It seemed to us that working with money, both in selling and buying, requires knowledge of arithmetic. We decided to compare children's performance in two types of situation: in schoollike tasks (computation exercises and problem solving) and outside-school situations, natural (street-vending) and simulated (a pretend shop). (For a summary of these studies, see Nunes, Schliemann, and Carraher, 1993.) The differences in performance by the same individuals in the same ability were replicated. The children performed significantly better on outside-school tasks, real or simulated, than on computation exercises. In both studies, word-problem performance was more similar to outside-school performance than to that observed in computation exercises.

Further, qualitative analyses showed that most of the time the children used different strategies for solving word problems and those from the outside-school setting, on one hand, and computation exercises, on the other. Computation exercises were, in the majority of cases, solved through typical school algorithms: numbers were written down and computation was carried out from right to left. Outside school, written algorithms were not used at all in real situations and not very often in the simulated shop, where computation was carried out most of the time through oral methods. More word problems were solved through oral than written methods. Oral calculation proceeded as a rule from hundreds to tens to units, the opposite direction from written algorithms, and worked with quantities (for example, 200, 50, and so on) rather than digits (for example, 2, 5, and so on). (For further discussion of arithmetic practices, see Nunes, Schliemann, and Carraher, 1993; Reed and Lave, 1981.)

We considered several alternative explanations in trying to understand these results. A first and most obvious one was that the situation as such affected performance. Children could have been more anxious doing the schoollike task than doing the outside-school task because they had associated school with failure in their past experience. A second possibility was that level of motivation differed between selling activities in the streets and solving schoollike tasks. A third possibility was that the children could think only in "concrete" terms and thus did better when props were available to be manipulated during problem solving. (To be honest, we did not believe in this last alternative hypothesis, but it was often presented to us when we talked with others about the results of these studies.) Any of these hypotheses would have protected the notion that individuals *have* abilities. But contradicting all of these explanations were two findings: (1) the children's performance in word problems, a school task solved without concrete materials, was more similar to their performance in outside-school tasks than to their performance in computation exercises; (2) when problem-solving procedure, oral versus written, was statistically controlled for, the differences in performance across situation disappeared.

Our next effort was to analyze oral arithmetic procedures in diverse ways to verify whether they rested on logico-mathematical principles that differed from those required for written arithmetic. Perhaps one needs to know fewer principles in order to carry out computations in the oral mode than in the written mode, we thought. If this happened to be true, we could still salvage the notion that children either have or do not have abilities; the set of abilities needed for oral arithmetic would differ from that needed for written arithmetic. But this hypothesis had to be rejected. When oral and written arithmetic were examined in terms of the mathematical properties they implicitly used, the properties turned out to be the same. In both oral and written calculation, addition and subtraction were based on the property of associativity, and multiplication and division were based on distributivity. Instead of being described by a smaller set of principles, oral arithmetic involved a larger set than written arithmetic. For example, oral subtractions were often solved by using addition as the inverse operation; instead of subtracting, for example, 95 from 168, some children subtracted 100 and then added 5 to this intermediary result. There is in the written algorithm for subtraction taught in Brazil no use of addition as the inverse operation.

In summary, these results showed (1) that children who were clearly competent in arithmetic when solving problems orally could be quite bad at solving the same problems through written procedures and (2) that the knowledge of both sets of procedures could be described on the basis of the same logico-mathematical principles. Furthermore, simple explanations in terms of situational or motivational effects did not fit the data. The differences in children's competence in arithmetic across modes of solution, oral versus written, were genuine, not a matter of false negatives in the schoollike tasks. The children were themselves often aware of this difference, and remarks such as, "I don't know how to do it on paper; I can do it only in my head," were not uncommon. A different way of thinking about the development of children's mathematical understanding was required.

Development of Mathematical Concepts as the Learning of Cultural Practices

A new starting point for the analysis of these results was found in the socio-historical view of development. Instead of assuming that nature sets a pattern, which is then simply nurtured by culture, we can assume that the pattern set by nature is much less specific than has been proposed in many theories. Nature's pattern, as Hinde (1991) has suggested, must have been set up a very long time ago under evolutionary pressures that do not resemble current socio-cultural conditions. Nature's pattern involves both specific constraints—such as the limits of perception and memory, for example—and much less specific possibilities, such as the human capacity for symbolically mediated action, as suggested by Luria (1973) and Vygotsky (1978). Higher psychological functions are distinguished from basic functions because they are carried out through symbolically mediated actions. The symbols we use in mathematics are learned through our participation in cultural practices. Below I discuss the cognitive and social aspects of participation in different cultural practices that involve mathematics.

Cognitive Aspects of Cultural Practices. Symbolically mediated actions surpass the limits of the simple functions. An example can be found in measurement. The accuracy of our perception and memory of lengths of objects is limited. If we were not capable of mediated knowledge of length, we would never be able to go to a shop and buy the exact amount of material we need to make a curtain. Measurement systems are cultural solutions to these limits in our perception and memory. When we master the measurement systems in our culture, they become an essential part of our ability to estimate quantities. As Gay and Cole (1967) have long demonstrated, people are not simply good or bad at estimating. For example, the Kpelle of Liberia were good at estimating distances in hand and arm spans, measurements that they often used in every-day life, but bad at estimating in foot lengths, a permissible but seldom used measure in their culture. The errors of Kpelle illiterate adults in estimation tasks where the distances varied between 72 and 180 inches were on the average not larger than 30 percent of the distances when they estimated in arm lengths. In contrast, when they estimated the same distances in foot lengths, their estimations were consistently more than 40 percent off, with average errors for certain distances being as high as 80 percent overestimation.

Symbolic systems do not merely express the reasoning we carry out in some other fashion; they are an essential part of the reasoning process itself. As pointed out by Scribner and Cole (1981), they structure thinking activities in the same way that the activities of tilling by hoe and tilling by tractor are structured differently. To continue the analogy, the hoe and the tractor afford different power to the farmer who tills the soil, and distinct symbolic systems afford distinct power to the subject who uses them. Nevertheless, the function carried out with different tools is still the same function. It is the goal of the activity that identifies the function.

Do oral and written approaches to arithmetic structure thinking differently, then? Nunes, Schliemann, and Carraher (1993) have compared the ways in which oral and written arithmetic differ in their organization. Written arithmetic works through procedures that distance it from meaning. Once the numbers are written down, algorithms are carried out in a digit-by-digit fashion, without concern for whether a digit is in the place of units, tens, or hundreds. This distance from meaning is an advantage, because it affords generality: the reasoning is the same for all values within the system, including decimal fractions. The advantage in terms of avoiding memory overload is also clear: there is little to be remembered across digits (only what was carried or borrowed) beyond the procedure itself. But the loss of meaning constitutes a disadvantage as well. The problem itself is often forgotten, and the meaning of the situation ceases to be used in monitoring the manipulation of the representations. Meaningless answers to problems in spite of correct step-by-step calculation are accepted in written arithmetic by significant numbers of students. One often quoted example (Carpenter, Lindquist, Mathews, and Silver, 1983, in Shoenfeld, 1988) comes from thirteen-year-old students in a National Assessment of Educational Progress conducted in the United States. One problem on the assessment stated that 1,128 soldiers were to be transported in buses that held 36 soldiers each and asked how many buses were needed for the transportation. Of the 45,000 students who were tested, 70 percent correctly performed the division but 47 percent incorrectly gave the figure 31 for their answer (with 29 percent answering "31 remainder 12" and 18 percent simply giving the figure 31).

In contrast to written arithmetic, oral procedures place greater demands on memory, and thus it is difficult for oral arithmetic users to deal both with numbers that have many digits and with long lists of numbers. However, oral arithmetic preserves the meaning of the problem throughout calculation and allows for better monitoring of the answers. Hundreds are treated as hundreds, tens as tens, and units as units, and references are often made to the content of the problem. These references are particularly clear in two-variable problems that involve multiplication and division. One example from Grando (1988), cited in Nunes, Schliemann, and Carraher (1993, p. 61), is presented below—the response of a farmer who was asked to calculate how many tea bushes were needed to fully plant an area sixty meters by thirty meters. The farmer was given the information that the spaces between the bushes had to be three meters by four meters.

> FARMER: Because in each four meters you plant one bush. Then ten bushes will give you forty meters, but there are still twenty meters to plant. Then you need five more bushes. It's four times five, twenty. Then it is fifteen bushes per row.
>
> RESEARCHER: Right, fifteen per row.
>
> FARMER: Then there are thirty meters on the side. Thirty by three. We'll see what else.
>
> RESEARCHER: I don't know what else.
>
> FARMER: Well, thirty by three is ten rows. Ten rows in the front by fifteen on the side. That's one fifty. Then it's right, it makes one hundred fifty bushes.

When computation is carried out with such clear monitoring for meaning, there is little room for meaningless answers.

The trade-offs between generality and meaning in oral and written arithmetic exemplify well the issues involved in the discussion of the power of symbolic systems. Each system is used for different purposes and specifies ways of thinking, structuring the subject's activity as it takes place.

It is likely that the way the system is learned also influences its knowledge and use later on. Although little detailed information can be found to help analyze this issue, an example from a study of negative numbers can be mentioned here.

Nunes (1993) compared the performance of children and adults in solving problems with negative numbers orally and in writing. (Participants were randomly assigned either to an oral or a written condition of testing.) The problems involved the addition or subtraction of debts and profits corresponding to a farmer's activities in one season, and subjects were asked to determine the farmer's situation at either the start or the end of the season. The values used in the problem were simple tens (for example, twenty, thirty, forty, and so on) so that arithmetic as such played a minimum role and reasoning about directed numbers could be the major issue. The participants in the study were likely to have been exposed to the oral arithmetic tradition and also had a history of learning written arithmetic; all were in school attending grades four to six.

Instruction on written arithmetic introduces the signs + and − as indications of which operation is to be carried out. Two different operations, addition and subtraction, cannot be carried out at the same time. Instruction on negative numbers conflicts with this previous practice, because the signs refer to the numbers (which for that reason are also called "directed" numbers), not to the operations. Within this second system of meanings, + and − can be used in the same operation. Thus there is discontinuity in the written practice but not in the oral practice.

Significant differences in performance were observed as a function of oral or written condition of testing, whereas no effect of grade level or age was found. Subjects who were tested in the oral mode performed significantly better than those tested in the written mode. Subjects in the written condition were often able to realize that their written solutions were wrong and recognized that they knew how to solve those problems only in their head—rather like the children in previous studies.

In a second study, Nunes (1993) was able to show that the differences across conditions of testing could be eliminated by a simple manipulation that allowed subjects to integrate the written symbols into their oral reasoning by stressing the meanings in the situation rather than the subjects' previous conceptions of how the written symbols should be used. The same subjects were tested twice, once in the oral and once in the written condition of testing (with approximately one week of interval between the two testing sessions). In the written condition of testing, subjects were given the problems written one per page and told that these were notes taken by a farmer about his profits and debts with different products during a season. Because he did not know how to write, the farmer marked his profits with a plus sign and his losses and debts with a minus sign. The subjects' task was to figure out the missing information, which could be the farmer's financial situation either at the beginning or at the end of the season. There were thus problems involving the addition of directed numbers (when the situation at the end of the season was missing) and subtraction problems (when the situation at the beginning of the season was missing). The problems were the same across the conditions of testing; only the mode of presentation—oral or written—differed.

In this second study, there were no significant differences across conditions of testing. However, the subjects in the written condition in this second study performed clearly better than those in the first study. By eliminating differences across conditions of testing, this simple manipulation demonstrated that the subjects' difficulties in the written condition could not be viewed as resulting from their not *having* the ability to solve problems in the written mode. Rather, the tradition of using signs that they had previously learned structured their activity in a way that interfered with problem solving.

In summary, the sociohistorical view of intellectual development proposes that the contributions of nature to development involve both specific constraints (such as perceptual and mnemonic limits) and possibilities (such as the ability to use symbols). The realization of these possibilities of symbol use may differ across situations, cultures, and time. Symbolic tools shape intellectual activity in much the same way as physical tools shape work practices. The powers and limits of distinct symbolic tools are reflected in people's reasoning activity, but they must not be confounded with the powers and limits of the users themselves. In other words, individuals who share the same reasoning principles about arithmetic may structure their problem-solving activity differently as a consequence of using distinct systems of representation. The differences in problem-solving activity are not individual differences; they can be observed across individuals but also within individuals under different circumstances.

Social and Personal Aspects of Cultural Practices. Although some progress seems to result from the idea that symbolic systems structure mental activity, there are still many gaps in our understanding of children's use of oral and written arithmetic. Two questions will be singled out here. First, why did the children in our studies try to use written arithmetic if they are so much better in oral procedures? Second, why did they fail to learn written arithmetic if it does not involve reasoning principles that are beyond the knowledge of arithmetic they already have? These issues will be addressed below.

School and Street Mathematics as Different Activities. Why do children who are competent in solving arithmetic problems in one way fail to use these successful methods in other situations? The problem here is to explain children's failure to maximize their success in a situation in which success is so important—that is, in school. Some time ago, I sketched a tentative answer to this problem by considering the characteristics of solving problems in and out of school (Nunes Carraher, 1990) in the same way that Scribner (1986) had already compared solving problems in life versus in an experimental situation. My suggestion was that the activities were themselves distinct because they were actually serving different social functions.

In school, children perform not to solve a problem they are interested in but to display knowledge. The particular nature of school discourse, and the ambiguities that result from a form of discourse where questions do not reveal an interest in the answer, have already been amply discussed in the literature (see, for example, Hammersley, 1977).

In contrast, when children solve arithmetic problems outside school, they have an investment in the situation; they want to know the answer because it will be used to make decisions (How much should I pay? How much change should I give? Did I get the right amount of change?). The differences in goals define different social functions. If written arithmetic is viewed not as a means but as a goal in school, children may not be willing to use their street knowledge of arithmetic in school.

However, this is not the whole story. The choice of the symbolic system used in school is not freely determined by the children. Although calculation can be carried out in either oral or written fashion, school practices require children to perform in the written mode most of the time, and this requirement includes calculation. With respect to arithmetic, teachers attempt to repress certain methods in the classroom (for example, counting on fingers) and systematically ignore others (for example, oral arithmetic practices: an answer not showing the written steps often either gets only partial credit or is viewed as the likely result of copying from the neighbor). The teachers' behavior validates written algorithms in arithmetic as good knowledge and fails to validate oral arithmetic (Edwards and Mercer, 1987).

This social demand is rooted in practical reasons, as is often pointed out by teachers, who have to check on the responses produced by many pupils at the same time. But it is likely that tradition is just as important, if not more so. Cole (1990) describes how schools as we think of them today originated in the teaching of cuneiform writing to scribes, a learning process that required long and systematic study. "Societies began to support young men who otherwise might be engaged directly in a trade or farming with the explicit purpose of making them 'scribes', people who could write. The places where young men were brought together for this purpose were the earliest schools" (p. 95). According to Cole, many of the characteristics of these early schools are still present in modern schools: characteristics such as the engagement in activities of copying and memorizing lists and facts, and learning removed from the contexts of practical activity. This latter characteristic entails focusing on skills (that will later become means) as goals of schooling.

Cultural Practices and Personal Identity. Why do children who know so much oral arithmetic fail to learn written arithmetic? How can we explain children's lack of success in mastering a schooled form of knowledge when the children understand the principles on which it is based?

Further reflection about the concept of cultural practices suggests that cultural practices extend their effects beyond the definition of social functions and activities. According to Ortner (1984), acting units in cultural practices are individual actors, whether historical individuals or social types such as "women," "workers," and so on. Social types are often identified on the basis of their participation in some cultural activity. "Scribes," "street vendors," "pupils," "teachers," "farmers," and so on are all social types defined in terms of such participation.

De Abreu (1994) has recently suggested that participation in oral arithmetic practices defines children's identities in ways that may influence their success or failure in school. Some of these social identities may be conceived as incompatible: for example, being a rural worker and succeeding in school. Thus children (along with their parents) who see no other future identity for themselves but being a rural worker come to reject school knowledge as not effective in practice, whereas those who start out well in school and seek a new identity do not value what they call "practical knowledge"—that is, oral arithmetic that works well for everyday needs.

De Abreu interviewed school children and teachers in a rural area in the northeast of Brazil about their concepts of school success and the use of oral and written arithmetic procedures. (De Abreu actually refers to home and school arithmetic, but she is considering the same type of practice we have been discussing; for the sake of consistency in this chapter, I will continue referring to oral and written procedures.) The teachers' interviews revealed that teachers were not unaware of the existence of oral arithmetic practices. They knew that farmers who had not attended school were able to calculate and solve their everyday problems involving numbers. They also recognized that the answers provided through oral calculations were accurate (and one teacher was even ready to recognize that farmers' oral methods could be more efficient and accurate than her own in practice). However, they did not include oral arithmetic in the classroom. As one of the teachers expressed, why teach the children these methods when what they need to know in order to succeed in school and ascend the social ladder is written arithmetic?

The children's interviews revealed that the children, when shown pictures of people farming, working in a supermarket, working in an office, and working in a street market, were more likely to see people working in the supermarket and the office as using mathematics and having been successful in school than people farming or working in a street market. As one of the children noted, if the rural worker had been successful in school, he would have had a better job.

The children also described their own participation in mathematical practices outside school. Different levels of participation were observed. Some children, for example, carried out purchases for the family and knew the prices of the items they bought and how to calculate totals and change in the shops. Other children, in their outside-school activities, simply worked as carriers of money and merchandise and tried neither to know the price of items they routinely bought nor to calculate the total price and the change.

Of the twenty children interviewed by de Abreu, nine were described as having little engagement in outside-school mathematics. Seven of these were successful in school mathematics, according to their teacher's evaluation. In contrast, nine showed clear engagement in outside-school mathematics, and only two of these were successful in school. The remaining two children were neither engaged in outside-school arithmetic nor successful in school. De Abreu suggests that these findings lead to two conclusions. First, there is no cognitive developmental order in the acquisition of oral and written procedures. If written procedures were more sophisticated and rested on but went beyond oral procedures, the seven of the nine children who were successful in school should have been more able with oral arithmetic. Second, because the majority of the children who were more engaged in outside-school practices were not successful in school arithmetic, she concludes that there may be a clash between the social identity suggested by the engagement in economic activities outside school (with the practical orientation it involves) and the learning of school arithmetic (viewed as less effective in everyday life but necessary for success in school).

De Abreu further emphasizes that written practices are perceived as allowing for social climbing. But the attempt to change from one social group to another comes with the possibility of rejection. Written arithmetic is not only taught but also tested for in school. Testing brings the possibility of failure. In contrast, neither rejection nor failure are contemplated outside school. The children already belong to the group of rural workers; thus rejection is not a possibility. Outside school there is no testing to threaten their participation in economic activities; if children need help when they start participating in economic activities, they can ask for it and will be helped by others. This host of social factors, she suggests, is likely to strengthen the engagement of some children in outside-school practices, whereas other children are encouraged to identify with school arithmetic and have restricted participation in arithmetic practices outside school.

In summary, cultural practices differ not only in their cognitive but also in their social characteristics. Oral and written arithmetic fulfill different social functions and are maintained apart both for practical reasons and as a consequence of tradition. Participation in cultural practices also conveys identification and attitudes. Rural workers and those who see themselves growing up to be rural workers do not need to know things that are good in theory; they need to be good in practice. Teachers do not need to teach oral arithmetic, because it is written arithmetic that will bring children success in school.

Conclusion

Much more work is still needed for a better understanding of the relationship between the development of intelligence and the mastery of different symbolic systems. It seems safe to conclude at this point that mastering new symbolic systems alters our possibilities in terms of mental activities. Different symbolic systems are more powerful for particular functions, and their users will be correspondingly enabled. I wish to suggest that we need, however, to prevent our psychological theories from taking the step from "enabled by a powerful tool" to "a more able individual." The language of individual differences signifies that differences are in the individual, not in the tools they use. It is, in my view, very unfortunate that in the long history of psychological testing in order to predict school achievement, psychology has slipped from testing for *knowledge* in schools to testing for *abilities*. However, the assumptions we accept about knowledge differ from those we accept about abilities. Whereas knowledge is culturally developed and transmitted, abilities are assumed to result from an interaction between nature and nurture, and nature cannot be radically transformed by nurture.

In summary, the conception that children develop their minds through the mastery of symbolic tools learned in the context of cultural practices can offer a plausible explanation for within-individual differences, a type of finding in psychology that cannot be explained by the notion of individual ability.

References

Carraher, T. N., Carraher, D. W., and Schliemann, A. D. "Mathematics in the Streets and in Schools." *British Journal of Developmental Psychology,* 1985, *3,* 21–29.

Carraher, T. N., Carraher, D. W., and Schliemann, A. D. "Written and Oral Mathematics." *Journal for Research in Mathematics Education,* 1987, *18,* 83–97.

Cole, M. "Cognitive Development and Formal Schooling: The Evidence from Cross-Cultural Research." In L. C. Moll (ed.), *Vygotsky and Education.* New York: Cambridge University Press, 1990.

Cole, M., Gay, J., Glick, J., and Sharp, D. *The Cultural Context of Learning and Thinking.* New York: Basic Books, 1971.

de Abreu, G. "Understanding How Children Experience the Relationship Between Home and School Mathematics." Unpublished doctoral dissertation, Department of Education, University of Cambridge, 1994.

Donaldson, M. *Children's Minds.* Glasgow, Scotland: Fontana, 1978.

Edwards, D., and Mercer, N. *Common Knowledge: The Development of Understanding in the Classroom.* London: Routledge, 1987.

Gay, J., and Cole, M. *The New Mathematics and an Old Culture: A Study of Learning Among the Kpelle of Liberia.* Troy, Mo.: Holt, Rinehart & Winston, 1967.

Greenfield, P. "On Culture and Conservation." In J. S. Bruner, R. R. Oliver, and P. M. Greenfield (eds.), *Studies in Cognitive Development.* New York: Wiley, 1966.

Hammersley, M. "School Learning: The Cultural Resources Required by Pupils to Answer a Teacher's Question." In P. Woods and M. Hammersley (eds.), *School Experience.* London: Croom Helm, 1977.

Hinde, R. A. "A Biologist Looks at Anthropology." *Man,* 1991, *26,* 583–608.

Labov, W. "The Logic of Non-Standard English." In F. Williams (ed.), *Language and Poverty.* Chicago: Markham, 1970.

Lave, J. *Cognition in Practice: Mind, Mathematics, and Culture in Everyday Life.* New York: Cambridge University Press, 1988.

Luria, A. *The Working Brain: An Introduction to Neuropsychology.* Harmondsworth, U.K.: Penguin, 1973.

Nunes, T. "Learning Mathematics: Perspectives from Everyday Life." In R. B. Davis and C. A. Maher (eds.), *Schools, Mathematics, and the World of Reality.* Needham Heights, Mass.: Allyn & Bacon, 1993.

Nunes Carraher, T. "Negotiating the Results of Mathematical Computations." *International Journal of Educational Research,* 1990 *13,* 637–646.

Nunes Carraher, T., and Schliemann, A. D. "Fracasso Escolar: Uma Questão Social." *Cadernos de Pesquisa,* 1983, *45,* 3–19.

Nunes, T., Schliemann, A. D., and Carraher, D. W. *Street Mathematics and School Mathematics.* New York: Cambridge University Press, 1993.

Ortner, S. B. "Theory in Anthropology Since the Sixties." *Comparative Studies in Sociology and History,* 1984, *26,* 126–166.

Perret-Clermont, A. N. *Social Interaction and Cognitive Development in Children.* San Diego, Calif.: Academic Press, 1980.

Reed, H. J., and Lave, J. "Arithmetic as a Tool for Investigating Relations Between Culture and Cognition." In R. W. Casson (ed.), *Language, Culture, and Cognition: Anthropological Perspectives.* New York: Macmillan, 1981.

Scribner, S. "Thinking in Action: Some Characteristics of Practical Thought." In R. J. Sternberg and R. K. Wagner (eds.), *Practical Intelligence: Nature and Origin of Competence in the Everyday World.* Cambridge, Mass.: Harvard University Press, 1986.

Scribner, S., and Cole, M. *The Psychology of Literacy.* Cambridge, Mass.: Harvard University Press, 1981.

Shoenfeld, A. H. "When Good Teaching Leads to Bad Results: The Disasters of Well-Taught Mathematics Courses." *Educational Psychologist,* 1988, *23,* 145–166.

Vygotsky, L. S. *Mind in Society.* Cambridge, Mass.: Harvard University Press, 1978.

TEREZINHA NUNES is lecturer in child development at the Institute of Education in London.

Conceptual ambiguities surrounding the concept of cultural practices, indexed by the use of such allied terms as activity, context, *and* situation, *are discussed in terms of their historical origins and implications for current research and theory.*

The Supra-Individual Envelope of Development: Activity and Practice, Situation and Context

Michael Cole

The past two decades have seen many changes in approaches to cognitive development, but none more profound than the current popularity of the notion that some unit of analysis larger than, but inclusive of, the individual is required if we are to attain a more adequate conception of the processes at work. The crucial questions then become, What is this unit of analysis? How is it to be described? How, if we abandon the individual as the unit of psychological analysis, are we to go about collecting data with which to evaluate our theories and guide our practice?

The essays in this volume all contribute to answering these questions. They are united by the idea that "cultural practices" offer the needed unit of analysis. However, when one delves into the individual chapters, it quickly becomes apparent that *practice* is an extremely polysemous concept; it seems to inhabit a common semantic space with such concepts as *activity, context, situation,* and *event.*

Barbara Rogoff, Jacqueline Baker-Sennett, Pilar Lacasa, and Denise Goldsmith, for example, talk in their chapter about a unit of analysis that appears to be an amalgam of the concepts *practice, activity,* and *event:* "We make use of 'activity' or 'event' as the unit of analysis, with active and dynamic contributions from individuals, their social partners, and historical traditions and materials and their transformations." From later citations in their chapter (to Dewey and Pepper, for example), we can see links between their formulations and American pragmatist thinking relevant to cultural practices theory.

Barbara Miller also conceives of cultural practices as closely related to activity. She writes that "'practices' are taken here to be people's routine activities, which are inextricably linked both to the [societal] structures within which actors operate and to the meaning that actors give to their activities. In themselves, practices contain both structure and meaning in some sense, and they are the basis for transformation and change in structure and meaning. Practices are the everyday pivot between structure and the individual." Later in her chapter, she suggests listening to music as an example of a secular practice and meditation as a religious practice. Both listening to music and meditation fit most everyday definitions of an activity.

Terezinha Nunes also treats *practice* and *activity* almost as if they were synonyms. She writes that "symbolic tools shape intellectual activity in much the same way as physical tools shape work practices. . . . In other words, individuals who share the same reasoning principles about arithmetic may structure their problem-solving activity differently as a consequence of using distinct systems of representation." Later in her chapter, while discussing cultural practices and personal identity, she asserts that "social types are often identified as a consequence of their participation in some cultural activity."

Richard Shweder, Lene Arnett Jensen, and William Goldstein do not offer a definition of the term *practice* in their chapter, but in specifying what they take to be a cultural account of mind, they emphasize that "one must establish a correspondence between behavior patterns and the preferences, values, moral goods, and causal beliefs exhibited in those behaviors." Later, they comment that it is in the matrix of possibilities provided by cultural practices that the behaviors become symbolic actions rather than "mere behavior."

In spite of the diversity in their vocabularies and objects of analysis, we can discern convergence of the authors appearing in this volume on a unit of psychological analysis that includes not only the individual but also a supra-individual sociocultural entity that is the effective medium of uniquely human forms of being in the world. The big challenge is to attain greater precision in our ability to communicate about this unit of analysis and the forms of interaction by which individual psychological functioning and its socioculturally structured environment are intertwined.

To contribute to this effort, I will explore different attempts to specify the supra-individual unit of analysis in terms of which culture's contributions to human development are to be understood. I need to state at the outset that at the end of this inquiry I will not be able to differentiate and order the various ways of speaking about this supra-individual unit of analysis with logical precision. My more modest hope is that this historical exercise will make clearer the alternative vocabularies now in use for talking about culture and development and thereby promote dialogue on the developmental mechanisms at work.

Early Candidates for the Unit of Analysis: Situations and Contexts

My own attempts to talk about relations of culture and behavior display the same sliding back and forth between apparently related terms that is characteristic of the essays in this volume. As with Nunes, it was data generated by the application of standardized testing procedures among people living in sociocultural circumstances very different from my own that were the initial impetus for this effort. In attempting to understand why Kpelle (Liberian) rice farmers sometimes displayed a fine-tuned ability to use quantitative measurements and sometimes did not, John Gay and I (1967) appealed to the special role of measurement in particular economic activities. Later, in attempting to understand the checkered pattern of cultural differences in performance on a variety of specially contrived cognitive tasks, we proposed that "cultural differences in cognition reside more in the situations to which particular cognitive processes are applied than in the existence of a process in one cultural group and its absence in another" (Cole, Gay, Glick, and Sharp, 1971, p. 233).

Whatever the other virtues and shortcomings in such conclusions, they suffered from a key ambiguity: nowhere did we offer a definition of *activity* or *situation,* both of which we were using in a commonsense fashion. Similar problems beset our use of the term *context* (Laboratory of Comparative Human Cognition, 1983).

Had we been sufficiently educated in the history of our discipline, our efforts could have been considerably enhanced by consulting the discussion of situation and context to be found in John Dewey's *Logic* (1938). The first part of Dewey's discussion appears to provide support for our conclusions. He wrote that "what is designated by the word 'situation' is not a single object or event or set of objects and events. For we never experience nor form judgments about objects and events in isolation, but only in connection with a contextual whole. This latter is what is called a 'situation'" (p. 66).

Dewey went on to comment that psychologists are likely to treat situations in a reductive fashion: "By the very nature of the case the psychological treatment [of experience] takes a singular object or event for the subject-matter of its analysis" (p. 67). But, he wrote, "In actual experience, there is never any such isolated singular object or event; an object or event is always a special part, phase, or aspect, of an environing experienced world—a situation" (p. 67).

Dewey believed that isolating what is cognized from the course of life behavior is often fatally obstructive to understanding cognition. It is such isolation (typical of experimental procedures in psychological studies of cognition), he argued, that gives rise to the illusion that our knowledge of any object, be it "an orange, a rock, piece of gold, or whatever," is knowledge of the object in isolation from the situation in which it is encountered. When our objects are standardized cognitive tasks, Dewey's point translates into the conclusion that cognitive tasks cannot be specified independent of the context that helps to constitute them; tasks/objects/texts and *con*texts ("with-texts") arise together as part of a single process.

In short, we discover that there are two ways in which social scientists have thought about context. One treats context more or less as the "ground" upon which the "figure" of the object appears and tends strongly to treat context as prior to (and causal with respect to) the object/task. The other treats context and task/object as mutually constituted, such that causal priority cannot be assigned; figure and ground shift positions in the manner of a visual illusion. Both of these views have their champions and their uses.

Context as That Which Surrounds. When we retreat to Webster's dictionary to seek some clarity with respect to vocabulary, we find *context* defined as "the whole situation, background, or environment relevant to a particular event" and *environment* defined as "something that surrounds."

The notion of context as "that which surrounds" is often depicted as a set of concentric circles representing different "levels of context" that simultaneously constitute, and are constituted by, the levels above and below them. The psychologist's focus is ordinarily on the unit "in the middle," which may be referred to as an event or activity engaged in by individuals. The psychologist seeks to understand how this event is shaped by, and gives shape to, the broader levels of context.

This image is probably best known in connection with Bronfenbrenner's (1979) monograph on the ecology of human development. In applying this approach, Cole, Griffin, and Laboratory of Human Cognition (1987) took as the "unit in the middle" a teacher-pupil exchange that was part of a lesson that was part of a school day, and so on, and they discussed how its qualities were shaped by the organization of the classroom, the school as a whole, and the school's links to its community.

The notion of context as "that which surrounds," if treated in the proper fashion, provides one conceptual tool to grapple with the problem of how events at one "level of context" are shaped by events analyzed at neighboring levels. However, it also carries with it the danger that temporal and causal priority will be ascribed inappropriately to particular levels.

The study of language is an important domain in which the promise and problems of the idea of "layers of context" have been usefully explored (Bateson, 1972; Jackobson and Halle, 1956). A fundamental property of language is that its levels of organization are mutually constituted; a phoneme exists as such only in combination with other phonemes that make up a word. The word is the context of the phoneme. But the word exists as such—"has meaning"—only in the larger context of the utterance, which again "has meaning" only in relationship to a larger unit of discourse. As Bateson points out, "This hierarchy of contexts within contexts is universal for the communicational . . . aspect of phenomena and drives the scientist always to seek explanation in the ever larger units" (1972, p. 402).

Note that in this description there is no simple, temporal, ordering. "That which surrounds" occurs before, after, and simultaneously with the "act/event" in question. We cannot say sentences before we say words or words before synthesizing phonemes in an appropriate way; rather, there is a complex temporal interdependence among levels of context that motivates the notion that levels of context constitute each other.

To take our example of the teacher-child exchange, it is easy to see such events as "caused" by higher levels of context: teachers give lessons, which are events in classrooms, which are events in schools, and each lesson is structured according to conventions of the school a teacher works in, which are dictated by the board of education, and so on.

The difficulty with this top-down way of thinking about context is that it fails to capture the dynamic relationships between presumed levels, treating the context very much as if it were a stimulus or a cause. While more inclusive levels of context may constrain lower levels, they do not *cause* them in a unilinear fashion. For the event "a lesson" to occur, the participants must actively engage in a consensual process of "lesson making." Teachers often vary considerably in the way they interpret the conventions of the school, and school communities participate in the selection of the board of education. Without forgetting for a moment that the power relations among participants at different levels of context are often unequal, we must also remember that context creation is an active, two-sided process (see Chaiklin and Lave, 1993, for many relevant examples).

Context as That Which Weaves Together. When one delves into the history of the concept of context, one finds that it is derived from the Latin word *contexere,* "to weave together." Moreover, there is an intimate connection between context, interpreted as a process of weaving together, and the notion of an event. This connection is provided by Stephen Pepper in his analysis of contextualism as a worldview (what might currently be called a scientific paradigm).

Pepper (1942) suggests that the root metaphor underlying a contextualist worldview is the "historic event." By this, the contextualist does not mean primarily a past event—one that is, so to speak, dead and has to be exhumed. He means the event alive in its present. What we ordinarily mean by *history,* he says, "is an attempt to re-present events, to make them in some way alive again. . . . We may call [the event] an 'act,' if we like, and if we take care of our use of the term. But it is not an act conceived as alone or cut off that we mean; it is an act in and with its setting, an act in its context" (p. 232).

An "act in its context" according to Pepper and an object in its context/situation in Dewey's framework share the same basic characteristic: objects and contexts arise together as part of a single bio-social-cultural process of development. Pepper also writes about context in a way that invites us to think about it in terms of the alternative, "weaving together" conception. Events, he says, are described jointly by their quality and texture. But events are not to be broken down separately by quality and texture; rather, the event is what unites quality and texture, a whole greater than the sum of its parts. The holistic property is the quality; the parts or components make up the texture.

Although I am not aware of his using the metaphor of context as weaving, Gregory Bateson (1972) highlights the way in which mind is constituted through human activity involving cycles of transformations between "inside" and "outside" that are very similar to the idea of a two-sided relationship between strands and context in Pepper's writing. "Obviously," Bateson writes, "there are lots of message pathways outside the skin, and these and the messages which they carry must be included as a part of the mental system whenever they are relevant" (p. 458). He then proposes the following thought experiment: "Suppose I am a blind man, and I use a stick. I go tap, tap, tap. Where do I start? Is my mental system bounded at the hand of the stick? Is it bounded by my skin? Does it start halfway up the stick? Does it start at the tip of the stick?" (p. 459).

Bateson goes on to argue that such questions are nonsensical unless one is committed to including in one's analysis not only the man and his stick but his purposes and the environment in which he finds himself. When the man sits down to eat his lunch, the stick's relation to mind has totally changed, and it is forks and knives that become relevant. In short, because what we call *mind* works through artifacts, it cannot be unconditionally bounded by the head or even by the body but must be seen as distributed in the artifacts that are woven together and that weave together individual human actions in concert with and as a part of the permeable, changing events of life. The relevant order of context for analysis will depend crucially on the tools through which one interacts with the world, and these in turn depend upon one's goals and other constraints on action. According to this view of context, the combination of goals, tools, and setting (including other people and what Lave, 1988, terms "arena") constitute simultaneously the context of behavior and ways in which cognition can be said to be related to that context.

I will return to questions about situation and context presently, but first I need to bring the other central concepts in this discussion into focus.

An Alternative Duo: Activity and Practice

While the use of *situation* and *context* continues to be important in thinking about supra-individual units of analysis linking humans and their sociocultural worlds, in recent years this impulse has increasingly been expressed in terms of concepts such as *activity* and *practice,* which play a prominent role in the these chapters.

Contemporary ideas about the relation between cognition and practice can be traced at least back to the Greeks (Bernstein, 1971; Hickman, 1990). Aristotle distinguished three kinds of knowing: *theoria*—a form of contemplation; *praxis*—a form of practical activity (including political activity, business, and athletic performances); and *poeisis* (or *techne)*—a form of production such as that engaged in by craftsmen. These three ways of knowing were valued differently. Theoria was seen as a superior form of knowledge from which the two remaining forms of knowledge should arise, and praxis was seen as superior to techne.

When we see reflections of these distinctions among contemporary scholars for whom practice is an important organizing concept, it is often in the service of revaluing and reordering Aristotle's categories; in this tradition, praxis becomes not only the essential testbed of theory but the actual medium from which theory precipitates as a special moment of inquiry. The key figure providing a theoretical justification of this revaluation was Karl Marx, from whom the major contemporary practice theories are derived, through various historical intermediaries.

It is also probably fair to say that Marx is to blame for the confusion about how practice relates to activity in current academic discourse. The close pairing of these two terms is inscribed in the first of his "Theses on Feurbach" ([1845] 1967), where Marx wrote that "the chief defect of all materialism . . . is that the thing, reality, sensuousness, is conceived only in the form of the object or of contemplation, but not as sensuous human activity, practice, not subjectively. Hence in opposition to materialism the active side was developed by idealism—but only abstractly since idealism naturally does not know actual, sensuous activity as such" (quoted in Bernstein, 1971, p. 11).

From this passage, we are led to understand that Marx meant to retrieve the active individual from idealism and to rearrange the ontological separation among humans and artifacts as a way of superseding the dichotomy separating the material and the ideal. His formulation of the interpenetration of activity and practice and materiality/ideality is based on the assumption that "the object or product produced is not something 'merely' external to and indifferent to the nature of the producer. It is his activity in an objectified or congealed form" (Bernstein, 1971, p. 44). This activity "has the power to endow the material world with a new class of properties that, though they owe their origin to us, acquire an enduring presence in objective reality, coming to exist independently of human individuals" (Bakhurst, 1993, pp. 179–180).

Activity/practice emerges in this account as medium, outcome, and precondition for human thinking. It is in the territory of activity/practice that ideality emerges as a part of the dialect of development.

Twentieth-Century Theorists of Activity and Practice. I am incapable of mapping out all the major competing ideas about practice and activity in the twentieth century. Successful efforts to do so would have to encompass virtually all of modern social theory as expressed in many different national traditions and many social science and humanities disciplines. My more modest goal is to sketch out the genealogies that I judge to be most relevant to psychologists, based upon the references cited by contributors to this volume. They are relevant to different degrees and in different ways to the chapters in this volume, as I shall try to make clear.

Differing Traditions of Activity and Practice. One of the important "intermediaries" between Marx and contemporary practice approaches in the study of development is American pragmatism, present in this volume in the person of John Dewey. Dewey is, of course, the American philosopher who most emphasized the intimate relationship between practice and theory as the core of experience. Dewey also articulated a view of human activity that, as with Marx, emphasized the dependence of its quality on the contributions of prior generations and the nonidentity of human bodies and human minds:

"Experience does not go on simply inside a person. . . . In a word, we live from birth to death in a world of persons and things which is in large measure what it is because of what has been done and transmitted from previous human - activities. When this fact is ignored, experience is treated as if it were something which goes on exclusively inside an individual's body and mind. It ought not to be necessary to say that experience does not occur in a vacuum. There are sources outside an individual which give rise to experience" (Dewey, 1938, p. 39).

Dewey is also important to contemporary studies of development in terms of cultural practices because he provides a way of understanding the intimate linkages between cognition, practice, and participation in a community, a theme that has recently been brought to prominence through the writings of Jean Lave and her colleagues (Lave, 1988; Lave and Wenger, 1991). "Knowledge," Dewey wrote in a passage quoted in the chapter by Rogoff and her colleagues, "is a mode of participation, valuable in the degree in which it is effective. It cannot be the idle view of an unconcerned spectator" (Dewey, 1916, p. 393).

I find Dewey a constant source of inspiration when thinking about mind and activity as interconnected processes of development. But Dewey's descriptions of the systemic qualities to be sought when organizing activity for particular purposes (to reform the process of education, for example) are relatively abstract. What about the particular morphologies of particular practices? How does one organize the educational process around authentic experience in late-industrial capitalism?

A second line of influence on modern practice theorists comes via the Russian cultural-historical school of psychology, which started life as a way to formulate a psychology based upon Marxist ideas (Vygotsky, 1978; Van der Veer and Valsiner, 1991). Russians psychologists do not use the term *practice* when referring to the unit of psychological analysis; they speak instead of *activity,* and their tradition has come to be referred to as "activity theory" (Engeström, 1993; Leontiev, 1981; Wertsch, 1981).

Activity theory is anything but a monolithic enterprise. Within Russia there are at least two schools of thought about how best to formulate Marx's ideas in psychological terms (Brushlinskii, 1968; Zinchenko, 1985). In addition, there is a long German tradition of activity theory research (Raeithel, 1994), a Scandinavian/Nordic tradition (Engelsted, Hedegaard, Karpatscholf, and Mortenson, 1993; Engeström, 1987), and now, perhaps, an American tradition (Goodwin and Goodwin, in press; Nardi, 1994; Scribner, 1984). A good statement of the general tenets of this approach is provided by Engeström, who writes that an activity system "integrates the subject, the object, and the instruments (material tools as well as signs and symbols) into a unified whole. An activity system incorporates both the object-oriented productive aspect and the person-oriented communicative aspect of human conduct. Production and communication are inseparable (Rossi-Landi, 1983). Actually, a human activity system always contains the subsystems of production, distribution, exchange, and consumption" (1987, p. 67).

Engeström represents the complex set of relations that enter into an activity system in terms of the set of triangular relationships presented as Figure 6.1. At the top of the figure is the basic subject-mediator-object relationship familiar to developmental psychologists through the writings of Vygotsky and his colleagues. This is the level of mediated action through which the subject transforms the object to create outcomes. But action exists "as such" only in relation to the components at the bottom of the triangle. "Community" refers to those who share the same general object; "rules" refers to explicit norms and conventions that constrain actions within the activity system; "division of labor" refers to the division of object-oriented actions among members of the community. The various components of an activity system do not exist in isolation from each other; rather, they are constantly being constructed, renewed, and transformed as outcome and cause of human life.

Engeström echoes contemporary dissatisfaction with conceptions that treat contexts as "containers" of behavior, untouched in themselves by human actions, or as contained within interpersonal interaction. Jean Lave nicely summarizes the shortcomings of these two conceptions by declaring that "one has system without individual experience, the other experience without system" (Lave, 1988, p. 150).

Within the sort of activity theory characterization summarized in Figure 6.1, contexts are activity systems. The subsystem associated with the subject-mediator-object relationship exists as such only in relationship to the other elements of the system. This is a thoroughly relational view of context.

An important part of the activity theory approach is that it emphasizes that the process of development on the ontogenetic level is "co-constructed" with events at the level of activities. Moreover, just as the individual's history (ontogeny) is important to the analysis of change, so are the historically evolving changes in the bio-social-cultural forms called activities. One must seek to

Figure 6.1. Basic Structure of an Activity System According to Engeström

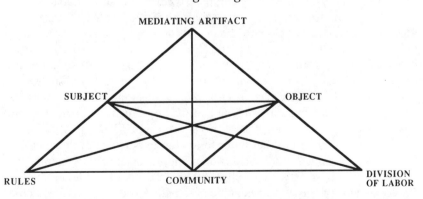

Note: At the apex of the triangle are the cultural artifacts mediating between subject and object. At the base of the triangle are the community, the division of labor, and the rules governing social life.

understand how human behavior contributes to changes in activity systems in addition to studying how particular systems of activity contribute to changes in individuals. It is this sort of concern that motivates Rogoff and her colleagues to include changes in technologies of calculation and communication as well as the active role that participants in earlier generations played in shaping the practices that young girls participate in today.

Nunes also uses concepts derived directly and indirectly from Russian cultural-historical psychologists in her exploration of experiential factors associated with arithmetic performance of Brazilian children from different social classes and occupational groups. She presents us with what appears to be an anomalous result. Virtually any theory linking culture and cognitive development can live with that brand of practice theory which rests on the proposition that "practice makes perfect." According to this way of reasoning, Brazilian children with a lot of arithmetic experience ought to develop their arithmetic knowledge. But, asks Nunes, how does it come to pass that children who know a good deal of oral arithmetic fail to learn written arithmetic? The answer is not to be found in declaring that there are social class differences in arithmetic ability; rather, one has to look to the ways in which mathematics enters the lives of children, to the cultural practices/activity systems in which they participate, and to the way that those supra-individual levels of structuration interact to produce the anomalous result.

With her assertion that "practices are the everyday pivot between structure and the individual," Barbara Miller introduces Western European social theory into the discussion of cultural practices. Her specific reference is to the ideas of Anthony Giddens (1979). With respect to human development, Giddens is concerned to avoid accounts of socialization that assume that the subject is determined by either the environment or by its "inherent characteristics." The first view, he writes, "reduces subjectivity to the determined outcome of social forces, while the second assumes that the subjective is not open to any kind of social analysis" (p. 120).

According to Giddens, practices (rather than roles, for example) are the basic constituents of the social system. They are also a unit of analysis that overcomes such dualisms as "individual versus social," which re-create one-sided accounts of development. The resolution of such dualisms, he claims (following Marx), is to be found at the level of practices: "In place of each of these dualisms, as a single conceptual move, the theory of structuration substitutes the central notion of duality of structure. By the duality of structure, I mean the essential recursiveness of social life, as constituted in social practices: structure is both medium and outcome of the reproduction of practices, and 'exists' in the generating moments of this constitution" (1979, p. 5).

Following Giddens, Miller looks to grooming practices to discover how the contested claims of traditional Indian Hindu society and contemporary middle-class U.S. society are resolved by adolescents from Indian families. "Choice of hair style" is a good example of something that is both the outcome of the reproduction of a practice (in that it results from decisions among a choice of alternatives that pre-exist in the practice) and the medium for the reproduction of the practice (in that it is from the varied current expressions of the practice that "next choices" are drawn).

Another important European thinker contributing to contemporary ideas of practice is anthropologist-sociologist Pierre Bourdieu (1977), who also seeks to block simplified notions of context as cause and whose work is also aimed at overcoming dualistic theories of cognition and social life. Bourdieu warns against theories that "treat practice as a mechanical reaction, directly determined by the antecedent conditions." He simultaneously warns against "bestowing free will and agency on practices" (p. 73).

Central to Bourdieu's strategy for balancing these two unacceptable extremes is the notion of *habitus*: "a system of lasting, transposable dispositions which, integrating past experiences, functions at every moment as a matrix of perceptions, appreciations, and actions and makes possible the achievement of infinitely diversified tasks" (pp. 82–83). In Bourdieu's approach, habitus is the product of the material conditions of existence and the set of principles for generating and structuring practices. Habitus, as its name implies, is assumed to take shape as an implicit aspect of habitual life experiences. It constitutes the (usually) unexamined background set of assumptions about the world. It is, Bourdieu remarks, "history made nature" (p. 78). "The habitus is the universalizing mediation which causes an individual agent's practices, without either explicit reason or signifying intent, to be none the less 'sensible' and 'reasonable'" (p. 79).

It seems to me that the data of Richard Shweder and his colleagues on the relationship between culture and sleeping practices, although Shweder does not make the connection, bears a strong resemblance to Bourdieu's ideas about habitus and practice as well as Giddens's ideas about the duality of structure. For Shweder and his colleagues, "A culture is a way of life lit up by a series of morally enforceable conceptual schemes that are expressed and instantiated in practice." "Way of life" appears to be a reasonable proxy for habitus, while "expressing, instantiating, and enforcing" seem to capture the process of structuration.

Bourdieu's insistence that practices not be seen as a mechanical response to antecedent conditions (either material conditions or habitus) is echoed in Shweder's point that in Orissa there is no "locked in," fixed pattern determining who sleeps next to whom at night, despite well-defined cultural values that are expressed and realized through sleeping practices.

Shweder and his colleagues assert that to give a cultural account of behavior "one must establish a correspondence between behavior patterns and the preferences, values, moral goods, and causal beliefs exhibited in those behaviors"—all of which are constituents of what Bourdieu refers to as habitus. The locus where the constituents of mind merge, for both Bourdieu and Shweder (and colleagues), is practices.

Congeries of Terms Reconsidered

I have by no means adequately surveyed the range of scholarly efforts to refocus psychologists on a view of cognition that places cultural mediation at its center—a view that focuses on some form of sociocultural structured/structuring entity that includes active human beings as its unit of analysis. Acknowledging this shortcoming, I want to concentrate my remaining comments on the possible entailments of differences in choices among such terms such as *situation, event, practice, activity,* and *context,* as well as what those terms have in common.

In her provocative discussion of cognition in practice, Jean Lave (1988) provides a succinct summary of several themes uniting scholars interested in practice theory:

An emphasis on the dialectical character of the fundamental relations constituting human experience. (In Lave's terms, human agency is "partially determined, partially determining" [p. 16].)

A focus on experience in the world that rejects the structure and dynamics of psychological test procedures as a universally appropriate template.

A shift in the boundaries of cognition and the environment such that, in Lave's phrasing, cognition "is stretched across mind, body, activity and setting" (p. 18)—a perspective sometimes referred to as "distributed cognition" (Hutchins, 1991; Norman, 1991; Salomon, 1993).

Although their vocabulary is somewhat different, I believe the same points of agreement can be attributed to Dewey in his discussions of situation and to those context theorists (such as Bateson) who hold firmly to the conviction that it is essential to see an "action as part of the ecological subsystem called context and not as the product or effect of what remains of the context after the piece which we want to explain has been cut out from it" (Bateson, 1972, p. 338).

At the same time, I have come away from this exercise worried about treating *activity, practice,* and *context* as if they were synonymous, especially in light of the fact that these terms often go undefined. They are not always synonymous, although they may well often coalesce in human experience. In some cases, practices appear to be parts of activity systems; for example, distinct literate practices can be seen as elements in a variety of activity systems (as part of a bar mitzvah, the weekly shopping, or a courtship). Activity systems can also be seen as elements in a practice (the term "practice of law" implies involvement in courtrooms, boardrooms, libraries, and private conferences, all of which are analyzable in activity theory terms).

There also appear to be some differences in theoretical and methodological approaches associated with adherence to one or another vocabulary preference. Those associated with activity theory, for example, appear to place a relatively heavy emphasis on the notion that practice is an essential theoretical moment in their inquiry (in comparison to those who adopt practice theory terms). In this, they are more similar to Dewey than to Giddens or Bourdieu. An orientation to activity theory also seems to place a relatively heavy emphasis on historicity and development.

I am uncertain about the reasons for, and significance of, these differences. One circumstance I can note is that practice theory has been developed largely in anthropology and sociology, which have a long and troubled relationship to historical explanations and notions of development. Such notions have too often been used to justify European political domination and exploitation of other parts of the world. This same legacy renders problematic the testing of theories in practice: What could it possibly mean for an anthropologist to test out her ideas about ritual practices in a society of which she is not a member? Yet societies do differ in multiple ways related to their histories; consequently, theoretically motivated descriptions of complex, interactively accomplished events are routinely vulnerable to alternative descriptions without the benefit of empirical criticism.

Similar questions can be, and have been, raised about activity theory. In some of its interpretations, it has adhered rather closely to notions of historical progress that come perilously close to asserting that primitives think like children. And despite its claims to unifying theory in practice, the number of convincing examples of research remains small.

The contributions to this volume illustrate the promise of a more powerful framework for understanding the development of thought in culture. Fulfilling that promise will require an increased commitment to interdisciplinary research among psychologists, anthropologists, and others. Such work is needed, I believe, because it is the most likely way to bring greater stability and precision to our ideas about the supra-individual unit of analysis toward which so many are gesturing.

References

Bakhurst, D. *Consciousness and Revolution in Soviet Philosophy: From the Bolsheviks to Evald Ilyenkov.* New York: Cambridge University Press, 1993.

Bateson, G. *Steps to an Ecology of Mind.* New York: Ballantine Books, 1972.

Bernstein, R. J. *Praxis and Action: Contemporary Philosophies of Human Activity.* Philadelphia: University of Pennsylvania Press, 1971.

Bourdieu, P. *Outline of a Theory of Practice.* New York: Cambridge University Press, 1977.

Bronfenbrenner, U. *Experimental Human Ecology.* Cambridge, Mass.: Harvard University Press, 1979.

Brushlinskii, A. V. *Kul'turno-istoricheskaya teoriya myishleniya* (The cultural-historical school of thinking). Moscow: Vysshaya Shkola, 1968.

Chaiklin, S., and Lave, J. *Understanding Practice: Perspectives on Activity and Context.* New York: Cambridge University Press, 1993.

Cole, M., Gay, J., Glick, J. A., and Sharp, D. W. *The Cultural Context of Learning and Thinking.* New York: Basic Books, 1971.

Cole, M., Griffin, P., and Laboratory of Comparative Human Cognition. *Contextual Factors in Education.* Madison: Wisconsin Center for Educational Research, 1987.

Dewey, J. *Democracy and Education.* New York: Macmillan, 1916.

Dewey, J. *Logic: The Theory of Inquiry.* Troy, Mo.: Holt, Rinehart & Winston, 1938.
Engelsted, N., Hedegaard, M., Karpatscholf, B., and Mortenson, A. *The Societal Subject.* Aarhus, Denmark: Aarhus University Press, 1993.
Engeström, Y. E. *Learning by Expanding.* Helsinki, Finland: Oy, 1987.
Engeström, Y. E. "Developmental Studies of Work as a Testbench of Activity Theory: The Case of Primary Care Medical Practice." In S. Chaiklin and J. Lave (eds.), *Understanding Practice: Perspectives on Activity and Context.* New York: Cambridge University Press, 1993.
Gay, J., and Cole, M. *The New Mathematics and an Old Culture.* Troy, Mo.: Holt, Rinehart & Winston, 1967.
Gibson, J. *The Senses Considered as Perceptual Systems.* Boston: Houghton Mifflin, 1979.
Giddens, A. *Central Problems in Social Theory.* London: Macmillan, 1979.
Goodwin, C., and Goodwin, M. H. "Perception, Technology, and Interaction on a Scientific Research Vessel." *Social Studies of Science,* in press.
Hickman, L. *John Dewey's Pragmatic Technology.* Bloomington: Indiana University Press, 1990.
Hutchins, E. "The Social Organization of Distributed Cognition." In L. B. Resnick, J. M. Levine, and S. D. Teasley (eds.), *Perspectives on Socially Shared Cognition.* Washington, D.C.: American Psychological Association, 1991.
Jackobson, R., and Halle, M. *Fundamentals of Language.* The Hague, Netherlands: Mouton, 1956.
Laboratory of Comparative Human Cognition. "Culture and Cognitive Development." In W. Kessen (ed.), *Mussen's Handbook of Child Psychology.* Vol. 1. (4th ed.) New York: Wiley, 1983.
Lave, J. *Cognition in Practice: Mind, Mathematics, and Culture in Everyday Life.* New York: Cambridge University Press, 1988.
Lave, J., and Wenger, E. *Situated Learning: Legitimate Peripheral Participation.* New York: Cambridge University Press, 1991.
Lektorsky, V. A. *Subject, Object, and Cognition.* Moscow: Progress, 1980.
Leontiev, A. N. "The Problem of Activity in Psychology." In J. V. Wertsch (ed.), *The Concept of Activity in Soviet Psychology.* Armonk, N.Y.: Sharpe, 1981.
Marx, K. "Theses on Feurbach." In L. D. Easton and K. H. Guddat (eds.), *Writings of the Young Marx on Philosophy and Society.* New York: Doubleday/Anchor, 1967. (Originally published 1845.)
Nardi, B. (ed.). *Activity Theory and Human-Computer Interaction.* Cambridge, Mass.: MIT Press, 1994.
Norman, D. "Cognitive Artifacts." In J. Carroll (ed.), *Designing Interaction: Psychology at the Human-Computer Interface.* New York: Cambridge University Press, 1991.
Pepper, S. *Word Hypotheses.* Berkeley: University of California Press, 1942.
Raeithel, A. "Symbolic Reproduction of Social Coherence." *Mind, Culture, and Activity,* 1994, *1,* 69–88.
Rossi-Landi, F. *Language as Work and Trade: A Semiotic Homology for Linguistics.* South Hadley, Mass.: Bergin & Garvey, 1983.
Salomon, G. (ed.). *Distributed Cognition.* New York: Cambridge University Press, 1993.
Scribner, S. "Cognitive Studies of Work." *Quarterly Newsletter of the Laboratory of Human Cognition,* 1984, *6* (entire issues 1 and 2).
Van der Veer, R., and Valsiner, J. *Understanding Vygotsky: A Quest for Synthesis.* Oxford, U.K.: Blackwell, 1991.
Vygotsky, L. S. *Mind in Society.* Cambridge, Mass.: Harvard University Press, 1978.
Wertsch, J. *The Soviet Concept of Activity.* Armonk, N.Y.: Sharpe, 1981.
Zinchenko, V. P. "Vygotsky's Ideas About Units for the Analysis of the Mind." In J. V. Wertsch (ed.), *Culture, Communication, and Cognition: Vygotskian Perspectives.* New York: Cambridge University Press, 1985.

MICHAEL COLE is professor of communication and psychology at the University of California, San Diego.

CONCLUSION

We began this project with a particular purpose—one that we saw as especially apt for a time when references to social contexts are increasing in frequency and diversity. We wanted to introduce a concept, to demonstrate several of the ways in which it is being thought about and pursued in research, and to point to some propositions that cut across the variety.

We are well aware that the coverage has gaps: inevitable in a short volume with a strict page limit. (Every contributor concluded with a sense of important points foregone.) The temptation, then, in any final comment is to try to mention everything that has not yet been covered.

In the face of that impossibility, we shall end by noting a single new direction—one that flows from Michael Cole's commentary. He has pointed to the need for some integration of practice theories and activity theories. We see the need as well to bring together approaches that emphasize actions and approaches that emphasize meanings. These, too, lack integration. "Meanings" appear under the labels of belief systems, cultural models, folk theories, consensus models, social representations, explanatory styles, and the interpretation of practices (see, for example, D'Andrade and Strauss, 1992; Duveen and Lloyd, 1990; Harkness and Super, in press; Modell, 1994).

Lave (1993) has suggested that these two broad approaches to contextualizing development differ both in their emphasis and in their history. The first concentrates on the nature of engagement with an activity; its tradition is likely to be activity theory. The second "focuses on the construction of the world in social interaction" (Lave, 1993, p. 17); its tradition is likely to be phenomenological social theory. The contrast is provocative, and we join Lave in urging attention to both these approaches and to the continuing analysis of their interconnections and of what each contributes to the overarching problem of contextualizing development.

Jacqueline J. Goodnow
Peggy J. Miller
Frank Kessel
Editors

References

D'Andrade, R. G., and Strauss, C. *Human Motives and Cultural Models.* New York: Cambridge University Press, 1992.

Duveen, G., and Lloyd, B. (eds.). *Social Representations and the Development of Knowledge.* New York: Cambridge University Press, 1990.

Harkness, S., and Super, C. *Parents' Cultural Belief Systems.* New York: Guilford, in press.

Lave, J. "The Practice of Learning." In S. Chaiklin and J. Lave (eds.), *Understanding Practice: Perspectives on Activity and Context.* New York: Cambridge University Press, 1993.

Modell, J. "The Developing Schoolchild as Historical Actor." *Comparative Education Review,* 1994, *38,* 1–9.

JACQUELINE J. GOODNOW *is professorial research fellow, School of Behavioral Sciences, Macquarie University, Sydney.*

PEGGY J. MILLER *is associate professor, Department of Speech Communication and Department of Psychology, University of Illinois, Urbana-Champaign.*

FRANK KESSEL *is program director, Social Science Research Council, with major responsibility for the Committee on Culture, Health, and Human Development.*

INDEX

Abbott, S., 23, 28
Activity: and development, 45; and participation, 53; and practice, 6, 105–106, 110–115
Activity theory: and activity systems, 113–114; and cultural practices approach, 6; and developmental psychologists, 6; Engeström's view of, 112–113; Russian school of, 112–113; traditions of, 112
Adolescents: first- and second-order concepts of, 71; and mentors, 69; oppositional identity of, 68. *See also* Hindu adolescents
Advice columns, and parent-child co-sleeping practices, 24–25
African Americans: parent-child co-sleeping practices of, 23; teenage pressures of, 68. *See also* Minorities
Analysis: personal/interpersonal/community planes of, 42, 46, 61–62; and relevant order of context, 110. *See also* Unit of analysis
"Annual Cookie Sale," 49
Apprenticeship, and learning, 41
Atkin, R., 48
Azmitia, M., 69

Baizerman, S., 76
Baker-Sennett, J., 55, 56
Bakhurst, D., 111
Baranes, R., 89
Barry, H., 24
Basso, K. H., 11
Bateson, G., 108, 109, 116
Bauman, R., 8, 9
Bausano, M., 23
Bentley, A. F., 45, 54
Berger, P. L., 47
Bernstein, R. J., 110, 111
Bourdieu, P., 7, 19, 115
Brazelton, T. B., 21, 22, 28
Brazil, mathematical practices of children in, 91–94
Briggs, C. L., 8, 9, 10, 12
Bronfenbrenner, U., 108
Brumberg, J., 82–83
Bruner, J., 13, 41

Brushlinskii, A. V., 112
Budwig, N. A., 41
Burton, L. M., 68
Burton, R. V., 24, 28

Carhart, M. L., 50
Caro, H. T., 67
Carraher, D. W., 91
Carraher, T. N., 91
Carugati, F., 19
Caspi, A., 51
Cassell, P., 71
Caudill, W., 24, 25, 26, 28
Ceci, S. J., 89
Chaiklin, S., 109
Change: and alternatives, 68; individual, and participation, 41; organizational, and storage model of past events, 56; participation and cultural, 10–12; personal/interpersonal/community planes of, 42; rapid social, 12; social, and Girl Scout cookie sales, 52–53
Child development. *See* Development
Children: as active, 43; and adult values, 10; interdependence of, 54; mathematical problem solving of, 91–94; narrative development of, 11; participation of, 62; as producers of culture, 43; shaming of, 10; shaping the minds of, 14; and storytelling, 9, 11. *See also* Parent-child co-sleeping
Co-constitution, of individual/community development, 42
Cole, M., 6, 87, 89, 90, 92, 95, 99, 107
Community: children's participation in, 62; co-constitution of individual and, development, 42; individual transformation of, 45–46; and institutional settings, 47; plane of analysis, 46; processes, 47
Context: defined, 107; and development, 8–9, 13, 88, 119–120; and environment, 108; ground-figure conceptualization of, 107–108; and historic event, 109; and knowledge, 107; and language, 108; and situation, 107–108; and teacher-child exchange, 108–109; as that which surrounds, 108–109; as that which weaves together, 109–110

ORDERING INFORMATION

NEW DIRECTIONS FOR CHILD DEVELOPMENT is a series of paperback books that presents the latest research findings on all aspects of children's psychological development, including their cognitive, social, moral, and emotional growth. Books in the series are published quarterly in Fall, Winter, Spring, and Summer and are available for purchase by subscription and individually.

SUBSCRIPTIONS for 1995 cost $56.00 for individuals (a savings of 20 percent over single-copy prices) and $78.00 for institutions, agencies, and libraries. Please do not send institutional checks for personal subscriptions. Standing orders are accepted.

SINGLE COPIES cost $17.95 when payment accompanies order. (California, New Jersey, New York, and Washington, D.C., residents please include appropriate sales tax.) All orders will be charged postage and handling.

DISCOUNTS FOR QUANTITY ORDERS are available. Please write to the address below for information.

ALL ORDERS must include either the name of an individual or an official purchase order number. Please submit your order as follows:
   Subscriptions: specify series and year subscription is to begin
   Single copies: include individual title code (such as CD59)

MAIL ALL ORDERS TO:
   Jossey-Bass Publishers
   350 Sansome Street
   San Francisco, California 94104-1342

FOR SUBSCRIPTION SALES OUTSIDE OF THE UNITED STATES, contact any international subscription agency or Jossey-Bass directly.